JERRY D. T

M000100698

A
THOUGHTFUL
Tracing the
Final Footsteps
of Jesus
HOUR

Pacific Press®
Publishing Association

Nampa, Idaho | Oshawa, Ontario, Canada
www.pacificpress.com

Cover design by Gerald Lee Monks
Cover design resources from sermonview.com
Inside design by Kristin Hansen-Mellish

Copyright © 2014 by Pacific Press® Publishing Association
Printed in the United States of America
All Rights Reserved

Scriptures quoted are from the King James Version unless otherwise indicated.
Scripture quotations attributed to NCV are from *The Holy Bible, New Century Version®*. Copyright ©
1987, 1988, 1991 by Thomas Nelson, Inc. All rights reserved.

The author assumes full responsibility for the accuracy of all facts and quotations as cited in this book.

You can obtain additional copies of this book by calling toll-free 1-800-765-6955 or by visiting
http://www.adventistbookcenter.com.

Library of Congress Cataloging-in-Publication Data:
Thomas, Jerry D., 1959-
  A thoughtful hour : tracing the final footsteps of Jesus / Jerry D. Thomas.
      pages cm
  A devotional study guide based on The Desire of Ages and Messiah.
  ISBN 13: 978-0-8163-5020-9 (pbk.)
  ISBN 10: 0-8163-5020-5 (pbk.)
1. Jesus Christ—Passion. 2. Devotional literature. I. White, Ellen Gould Harmon, 1827–1915. Desire
of Ages. II. Title.
  BT431.3.T46 2014
  232.96—dc23
                          2013042845

December 2013

Contents

Foreword

Although it happened nearly fifty years ago, I remember it distinctly. It was one of those magnificent New England fall mornings with the red maples and yellow oaks ablaze in an array of color. I was a newly baptized Seventh-day Adventist and a freshman at Atlantic Union College.

As I sat in Machlan Auditorium listening to the sermon that Sabbath morning, I was deeply moved. I do not remember who the preacher was, but I do remember what he preached about. He uplifted Jesus as the world's loving Redeemer. He talked about Jesus as Savior and Lord, about grace and forgiveness, about the cross, and eternal life. Tears filled my eyes. I was not raised in the Adventist Church and was not used to hearing such grace-filled, life-changing sermons. I was moved by the Christ of the cross then, and I am still moved by the cross now.

The cross never gets old. We will study the depths of Christ's sacrifice through the eternal ages. Christ's love and redeeming grace is the heart of all revival. Recently, my wife, Ernestine, and I read through *The Desire of Ages* on the life of Christ together. It was a moving experience. Now in this book you hold in your hands, Jerry D. Thomas has masterfully captured the essence of the final chapters of *The Desire of Ages* and developed study guides to accompany his devotional thoughts. Each encouraging chapter is filled with hope. At a time when the Seventh-day Adventist Church is emphasizing revival, this material can be powerfully used by the Holy Spirit to make a difference.

What is revival? It is the reawakening of the spiritual longings of the soul. It is rekindling the fires of faith. It is reigniting the heart's desire for the eternal. The most effective way to foster revival is by a deeper appreciation for the Christ of Calvary. Looking to Jesus on the cross, we are changed. Charmed by His grace and drawn by His love, the things of time take second place to the things of eternity. There is nothing more powerful to stimulate a spiritual revival than the cross. The cross is at the heart of all revival, it is at the center of all revival, and it is the object of all revival.

This is why I am so enthusiastic about *A Thoughtful Hour*. As you meditate on the life of Christ and consider its closing scenes, your own life will be changed. At the cross, a dying thief found forgiveness, and a hard-hearted Roman soldier was transformed. Millions have found hope at the cross through the centuries. Whether you are a committed Christian or you consider yourself a nominal believer, whether you are full of faith or have little faith, this book is for you. A deeper look at Jesus will strengthen your faith in ways that you cannot now imagine.

A Thoughtful Hour is not designed to be read quickly or casually. As the title implies, it is to be read thoughtfully. Read each powerful page with an openness of heart, while asking the Holy Spirit to impress the truths you read upon your heart. As you sense the Holy Spirit moving in your life while you review these pages, pause and meditate upon what you are reading. Ask God to do something special in your life. The purpose of this book is not to fill your head with facts. It is to lead you into an encounter with Jesus that is beyond what you can imagine.

It is my prayer that as you meditate upon these pages, Jesus' love will fill your life and you, too, will be filled with wonder at His amazing grace.

Mark A. Finley

Introduction

"It would be well for us to spend a thoughtful hour each day in contemplation of the life of Christ. We should take it point by point, and let the imagination grasp each scene, especially the closing ones. As we thus dwell upon His great sacrifice for us, our confidence in Him will be more constant, our love will be quickened, and we shall be more deeply imbued with His spirit. If we would be saved at last, we must learn the lesson of penitence and humiliation at the foot of the cross"
(*The Desire of Ages*, 83).

As precious as the story of Jesus is to each of us, our daily lives keep us so busy that it's hard to carve out the time we would like to spend learning about Him. It's hard to find an hour—a thoughtful hour—reading and studying the gospel accounts of His life.

That's why this book exists. It is designed to make that thoughtful hour easier, to give a little structure and focus to a study of the life of Christ. Whether you work through the pages as part of a group study or on your own, you will find a fresh look at the gospel story. The questions can be answered either as part of a discussion or in your own heart as you read in thoughtful consideration.

Each of us learns differently. Many of us have loved the heart-touching account of the life of Christ found in Ellen White's *The Desire of Ages*. Those poetic passages have lifted our minds to a higher level, opening before us the teachings of heaven and the struggles of life.

Others have struggled with the language level in *The Desire of Ages*. For that reason, this book includes selections from *Messiah*, the modern language adaptation of *The Desire of Ages*. The simpler vocabulary and shorter sentences and paragraphs have helped many grasp the scenes and lessons from Jesus' life as they have not been able to before.

As each chapter of this book opens, you will see which Scripture passages are referenced. You can also see which chapters of *The Desire of Ages* (and *Messiah*) tell the same story. From there, an introduction leads you into the study. You are encouraged to let your imagination grasp each scene as you grapple with what the disciples heard when Jesus spoke, what they thought, and what Jesus meant for them to learn.

Then you will be invited to "reflect on the story" as you read a selection from either *The Desire of Ages* or *Messiah*. "Questions to consider" follow this selection and invite you to review what you read, apply your imagination to the scenes, and apply what you read to your life today. A second selection to read will come from *Messiah*, with more questions to consider. Each selection will have the pages referenced from both *The Desire of Ages* and *Messiah,* so that you can read the version you choose.

In this book, we will focus on the "closing scenes" of Jesus' life, following His final footsteps to the cross and beyond. From the pen of inspiration we will glean lessons that can guide our lives today and lead us to a closer walk with Jesus than ever before.

In your personal or group study, you may find that you cover a chapter each day. Or you may find that some chapters lead to more reading and more discussion. Approach the study at your own pace and dwell on each story until the Holy Spirit has opened it to you with life-changing power. There is much more that could be read in Scripture and in the writings of Ellen White. There are many other questions that could be asked. Study until the questions in your heart are answered.

It is my prayer that in your "thoughtful hours," you will find that the story of Jesus' final days comes alive in your imagination. May the scenes of His sacrifice and His resurrection be as real and as life-changing to you as they were to those who witnessed it all in person.

Jesus' Last Journey   1

This study is based on Luke 9:51–10:24
and *The Desire of Ages*, chapter 53
—see also *Messiah*, chapter 53.

The turn toward Jerusalem

Jesus walked the roads and paths of Israel for three and a half years. From north of the Sea of Galilee, on both the east and west sides of the Jordan River, to Tyre and Sidon on the shore of the Mediterranean Sea, to the shores of the Dead Sea in the south, Jesus had covered the countryside. According to Matthew 9:35, "Jesus traveled through all the towns and villages, teaching in their synagogues, preaching the Good News about the kingdom, and healing all kinds of diseases and sicknesses" (NCV).

As Jesus traveled toward Jerusalem for the last time, He changed His method of working. Before this time, He had always tried to avoid publicity. He hushed those who praised Him and quieted anyone who declared that He was the Messiah. Sometimes He left towns before daylight so no one would know where He was headed. He tried to keep the crowd's expectations under control while He taught new truths about the kingdom of God.

Now His attitude toward publicity had changed. As He traveled toward Jerusalem, great crowds walked with Him. Announcements were sent ahead to the towns He would pass through, telling all that He was coming. Before, He had worked quietly—but now that He was headed for His own sacrifice, He invited attention.

As they traveled the countryside with Jesus, the disciples had longed for Jesus to go to Jerusalem, stand in the temple square, and declare Himself to be the Messiah. They wondered why Jesus hesitated. They were sure that the people would gather on His side, support His cause, and band together to drive out their enemies. They had begged Him to do so, sure that all of Israel would flock to follow Him.

But now they understood the depth of His enemies' hatred. Now they realized what would happen if Jesus should fall into their hands. They knew that the danger would increase with every footstep taken closer to Jerusalem.

The disciples would have done anything to stop Jesus from making this journey. They begged Him to turn back. Jesus could hear the fear and concern for Him in their voices. Knowing what lay ahead, it was hard for Jesus to lead His friends into so much misery.

Reflect on the story

"Satan was at hand to press his temptations upon the Son of man. Why should He now go to Jerusalem, to certain death? All around Him were souls hungering for the bread of life. On every hand were suffering ones waiting for His word of healing. The work to be wrought by the gospel of His grace was but just begun. And He was full of the vigor of manhood's prime. Why not go forward to the vast fields of the world with the words of His grace, the touch of His healing power? Why not take to Himself the joy of giving light and gladness to those darkened and sorrowing millions? Why leave the harvest gathering to His disciples, so weak in faith, so dull of understanding, so slow to act? Why face death now, and leave the work in its infancy? The foe who in the wilderness had confronted Christ assailed Him now with fierce and subtle temptations. Had Jesus yielded for a moment, had He changed His course in the least particular to save Himself, Satan's agencies would have triumphed, and the world would have been lost.

"But Jesus had 'steadfastly set His face to go to Jerusalem.' The one law of His life was the Father's will. In the visit to the temple in His boyhood, He had said to Mary, 'Wist ye not that I must be about My Father's business?' Luke 2:49. At Cana, when Mary desired Him to reveal His miraculous power, His answer was, 'Mine hour is not yet come.' John 2:4. With the same words He replied to His brothers when they urged Him to go to the feast. But in God's great plan the hour had been appointed for the offering of Himself for the sins of men, and that hour was soon to strike. He would not fail nor falter. His steps are turned toward Jerusalem, where His foes have long plotted to take His life; now He will lay it down. He set His face steadfastly to go to persecution, denial, rejection, condemnation, and death" (*The Desire of Ages*, 486; see also *Messiah*, 273, 274).

Questions to consider

1. Why did Jesus change His method of working as He neared the end of His ministry? What practical benefits did this change bring? What risks?

2. What temptation did Satan use against Jesus at this time? Would that temptation have appealed to you?

3. "The one law of His life was the Father's will." How would you describe the "law" of your life?

Reflect on the story

"Jesus sent messengers ahead to a Samaritan village to announce that He was coming. But these Samaritans hated the Jews and they refused to let Jesus stay there because He was going to the Jewish people in Jerusalem. Because of their prejudice, they missed out on the blessing He could have brought to their whole town.

"James and John were greatly insulted at this rude treatment. Seeing Mount Carmel in the distance, they were reminded of the story of Elijah and the prophets of Baal. 'Lord, do You want us to call fire down from heaven to destroy these people?' they asked.

"They were surprised at Jesus' sharp answer. 'You don't realize what kind of spirit you're speaking with. I didn't come to destroy people. I came to save them.'

"Jesus never forces people to accept Him. He accepts only the willing surrender of love. A desire to hurt others who don't agree with us or appreciate our work can only come from Satan. Nothing offends God more than when people try to harass or torment those who won't accept their religious views.

"Jesus spent a good portion of the final months of His ministry in Perea, the area across the Jordan from Judea. Here, with crowds following Him at every step, He repeated many of the things He had taught in other places. He sent out seventy other disciples—ones He had been teaching and training as they followed Him—to go two-by-two to the villages He would visit. Even after His rejection at the Samaritan town, Jesus directed the seventy disciples to visit the cities of Samaria first.

"Just before He returned to heaven, Jesus directed His disciples to Samaria as one of the first places they should preach His gospel. When they went to Samaria, the disciples found that the people there had been won over by Jesus' love. Many Samaritans joined their former enemies, the Jews, as they began the Christian church.

"When Jesus sent out the seventy disciples, He told them that if the people of a city wouldn't listen to them, they should shake the dust off their sandals and remind them that God's kingdom was coming. They weren't to do this out of anger or spite, but to show how serious it was to refuse to listen to Jesus' gospel. If the people rejected Jesus' message, they also rejected their Savior" (*Messiah*, 274, 275; see also *The Desire of Ages*, 486–489).

Questions to consider

1. Why did the Samaritans miss out on blessings Jesus could have brought? What attitudes or prejudices do we have that might make us miss out on blessings?

2. When is it right to respond with anger while defending God's cause?

3. If nothing offends God more than harassing those who won't accept our religious views, what should we do when others reject our message?

4. What might have been the result if Jesus had ignored or encouraged the disciples' anger at the Samaritans? Would they have neglected to share the gospel with the Samaritans after Jesus' return to heaven?

5. How do we reconcile the statement "Nothing offends God more than when people try to harass or torment those who won't accept their religious views" with His instruction that the disciples shake the dust off the sandals when leaving the cities of those who refused to listen?

Reflect on the story

"Then His mind reverted to the Galilean towns where so much of His ministry had been spent. In deeply sorrowful accents He exclaimed, 'Woe unto thee, Chorazin! woe unto thee, Bethsaida! for if the mighty works had been done in Tyre and Sidon, which have been done in you, they had a great while ago repented, sitting in sackcloth and ashes. But it shall be more tolerable for Tyre and Sidon at the judgment, than for you. And thou, Capernaum, which art exalted to heaven, shalt be thrust down to hell.'

"To those busy towns about the Sea of Galilee, heaven's richest blessings had been freely offered. Day after day the Prince of life had gone in and out among them. The glory of God, which prophets and kings had longed to see, had shone upon the multitudes that thronged the Saviour's steps. Yet they had refused the heavenly Gift.

"With a great show of prudence the rabbis had warned the people against receiving the new doctrines taught by this new teacher; for His theories and practices were contrary to the teachings of the fathers. The people gave credence to what the priests and Pharisees taught, in place of seeking to understand the word of God for themselves. They honored the priests and rulers instead of honoring God, and rejected the truth that they might keep their own traditions. Many had been impressed and almost persuaded; but they did not act upon their convictions, and were not reckoned on the side of Christ. Satan presented his temptations, until the light appeared as darkness. Thus many rejected the truth that would have proved the saving of the soul.

"The True Witness says, 'Behold, I stand at the door, and knock.' Revelation 3:20. Every warning, reproof, and entreaty in the word of God or through His messengers is a knock at the door of the heart. It is the voice of Jesus asking for entrance. With every knock unheeded, the disposition to open becomes weaker. The impressions of the Holy Spirit if disregarded today, will not be as strong tomorrow. The heart becomes less impressible, and lapses into a perilous unconsciousness of the shortness of life, and of the great eternity beyond. Our condemnation in the judgment will not result from the fact that we have been in error, but from the fact that we have neglected heaven-sent opportunities for learning what is truth" (*The Desire of Ages*, 489, 490; see also *Messiah*, 275).

Questions to consider

1. If the towns of Galilee will be judged more harshly than heathen towns, will Christians also be judged more harshly than atheists? Than Muslims or Buddhists?

2. Are we in danger of listening to others and holding on to our traditions instead of trying to understand God's Word for ourselves? How can we recognize this danger in ourselves?

3. How can we be sure that we heed the knock at our hearts? What might be the result if we do not?

Reflect on the story

"The most respected, the greatest and wisest men of that time, did not understand what Jesus was. But these fishermen and tax collectors knew. From time to time, when they were most open to the Holy Spirit, the disciples realized that God—dressed in the body of a human—was really standing with them. Often when Jesus taught them from the Old Testament—especially verses that pointed to Him, the Messiah—the disciples understood better than those who had written the words.

"The only way we improve our understanding of truth is to keep our hearts open to the Holy Spirit. Science is too limited to understand the plan of salvation. Philosophy cannot explain it. Salvation can be understood only by experience. Only a person who sees his or her own sinfulness can understand the precious value of the Savior" (*Messiah,* 276; see also *The Desire of Ages,* 494, 495).

Questions to consider

1. What is the only way salvation can be understood? What does this mean?

2. The greatest, most respected religious leaders of that time didn't understand who Jesus was. But simple fisherman did. What does this say to us today?

What Is God's Kingdom? 2

This study is based on Luke 17:20–22
and *The Desire of Ages*, chapter 55
—see also *Messiah*, chapter 55.

The kingdom of heaven

More than three years had passed since John the Baptist had announced, "The kingdom of heaven is here." Jesus had repeated the same claim many times. Now Jesus' enemies began to point out that nothing had changed. "Whatever his mission was, he failed," they declared to the people.

The leaders and most of the people in Israel were still expecting a warrior Messiah, a king who would lead them into battle and drive out the Romans. Their idea of a "kingdom of heaven" was a "kingdom on earth." It was clear that Jesus was not the leader they were looking for. They asked Him, "Where is this kingdom of heaven You keep talking about?"

Jesus' answer was unexpected. His enemies could not even begin to grasp it. "God's kingdom is coming, but not in a way that you will be able to see with your eyes. People will not say, 'Look, here it is!' or, 'There it is!' because God's kingdom is within you" (Luke 17:20, 21, NCV).

God's kingdom does not exist in another part of the universe or in another dimension. It is not something that happened in the distant past or will happen in the far future. God's kingdom is within us! Now, today!

You can see why the disciples had difficulty understanding this. It was a revolutionary concept—a reality-shifting paradigm. Even today, the most likely response to Jesus' answer is "What does that mean?"

How is it possible to live in God's kingdom while still being anchored to this earth? How can we live simultaneously in the world we see and in the world we cannot see?

The disciples had just begun to understand. Jesus said to them, "The time will come when you will want very much to see one of the days of the Son of Man. But you will not see it" (Luke 17:22). He wanted to tell them, "You do not realize what a great privilege you have had. You will look back and long for the days when you could walk and talk with the Son of God."

We can only imagine what it was like to walk and talk with the Son of God. But we can read the stories of those who did and, along with them, try to understand what Jesus was saying.

Reflect on the story

"It was not until after Christ's ascension to His Father, and the outpouring of the Holy Spirit upon the believers, that the disciples fully appreciated the Saviour's character and mission. After they had received the baptism of the Spirit, they began to realize that they had been in the very presence of the Lord of glory. As the sayings of Christ were brought to their remembrance, their minds were opened to comprehend the prophecies, and to understand the miracles which He had wrought. The wonders of His life passed before them, and they were as men awakened from a dream. They realized that 'the Word was made flesh, and dwelt among us, (and we beheld His glory, the glory as of the Only-begotten of the Father,) full of grace and truth.' John 1:14. Christ had actually come from God to a sinful world to save the fallen sons and daughters of Adam. The disciples now seemed, to themselves, of much less importance than before they realized this. They never wearied of rehearsing His words and works. His lessons, which they had but dimly understood, now came to them as a fresh revelation. The Scriptures became to them a new book.

"As the disciples searched the prophecies that testified of Christ, they were brought into fellowship with the Deity, and learned of Him who had ascended to heaven to complete the work He had begun on earth. They recognized the fact that in Him dwelt knowledge which no human being, unaided by divine agency, could comprehend. They needed the help of Him whom kings, prophets, and righteous men had foretold. With amazement they read and reread the prophetic delineations of His character and work. How dimly had they comprehended the prophetic scriptures! how slow they had been in taking in the great truths which testified of Christ! Looking upon Him in His humiliation, as He walked a man among men, they had not understood the mystery of His incarnation, the dual character of His nature. Their eyes were holden, so that they did not fully recognize divinity in humanity. But after they were illuminated by the Holy Spirit, how they longed to see Him again, and to place themselves at His feet! How they wished that they might come to Him, and have Him explain the scriptures which they could not comprehend! How attentively would they listen to His words! What had Christ meant when He said, 'I have yet many things to say unto you, but ye cannot bear them now'? John 16:12. How eager they were to know it all! They grieved that their faith had been so feeble, that their ideas had been so wide of the mark, that they had so failed of comprehending the reality.

"A herald had been sent from God to proclaim the coming of Christ, and to call the attention of the Jewish nation and of the world to His mission, that men might prepare for His reception. The wonderful personage whom John had announced had been among them for more than thirty years, and they had not really known Him as the One sent from God. Remorse took hold of the disciples because they had allowed the prevailing unbelief to leaven their opinions and becloud their understanding. The Light of this dark world had been shining amid its gloom, and they had failed to comprehend whence were its beams. They asked themselves why they had pursued a course that made it necessary for Christ to reprove them. They often repeated His conversations, and said, Why did we allow earthly considerations and the opposition of priests and rabbis to confuse our senses, so that we did not comprehend that a greater than Moses was among us, that One wiser than Solomon was instructing us? How dull were our ears! how feeble was our understanding!

"Thomas would not believe until he had thrust his finger into the wound made by the Roman soldiers. Peter had denied Him in His humiliation and rejection. These painful remembrances came before them in distinct lines. They had been with Him, but they had not known or appreciated Him. But how these things now stirred their hearts as they recognized their unbelief!

"As priests and rulers combined against them, and they were brought before councils and thrust into prison, the followers of Christ rejoiced 'that they were counted worthy to suffer shame for His name.' Acts 5:41. They rejoiced to prove, before men and angels, that they recognized the glory of Christ, and chose to follow Him at the loss of all things.

"It is as true now as in apostolic days, that without the illumination of the divine Spirit, humanity cannot discern the glory of Christ. The truth and the work of God are unappreciated by a world-loving and compromising Christianity. Not in the ways of ease, of earthly honor or worldly conformity, are the followers of the Master found. They are far in advance, in the paths of toil, and humiliation, and reproach, in the front of the battle 'against the principalities, against the powers, against the world rulers of this darkness, against the spiritual hosts of wickedness in the heavenly places.' Ephesians 6:12, R. V. And now, as in Christ's day, they are misunderstood and reproached and oppressed by the priests and Pharisees of their time" (*The Desire of Ages,* 507–509, see also *Messiah,* 281, 282).

Questions to consider

1. What does the statement "the kingdom of heaven is within you" mean to you? How does that truth change how you relate to people or to problems?

2. When did the disciples actually begin to understand Jesus' life and mission?

3. Can you imagine what might have been among the things Jesus wanted to say to the disciples but couldn't? What might He want us to know that isn't in the Bible?

4. The disciples allowed "earthly considerations and the opposition of priests and rabbis" to confuse them. Is there someone who might be confusing you so that you don't understand Jesus' teachings? Are you in danger of confusing someone else?

Reflect on the story

"The kingdom of God comes quietly and personally to human hearts. It is not flashy and demanding like the things of this world. Today many want to make Jesus the ruler of this world's governments, courts, and marketplaces. Since He isn't here in person, they feel free to speak for Him and try to enforce laws they think are His will. This is the kind of kingdom the Jews wanted when Jesus was here. But He said, 'My kingdom does not belong to this world.'

"The government Jesus lived under was dishonest and cruel. People were treated unfairly—even abused. But Jesus didn't try to reform or replace that government. He didn't speak out against the Romans or other national enemies. He didn't interfere with the authority of those who were in power. He kept out of government issues not because He didn't care but because the cure for those problems had to begin in the heart of each person.

"Jesus' kingdom isn't established by the decisions of courts or legislatures. It is set up by the influence of the Holy Spirit changing the hearts of humans. That is the only power that can truly change our society. And it is seen as we share the Word of God and show its power in our lives.

"Today, as it was in Jesus' day, God's kingdom is not with those who demand recognition and support by governments and civil laws. It is with those who live and share this spiritual truth: 'I was put to death on the cross with Christ, and I do not live anymore—it is Christ who lives in me' (Galatians 2:20, NCV)" (*Messiah*, 282, 283; see also *The Desire of Ages*, 509, 510).

Questions to consider

1. How does the kingdom of God come to human hearts? How did it come to your heart?

2. Should we speak for Jesus today, using His words, and try to enforce His laws in society around us? How does attempting to create a "Christian" nation today differ from the kind of kingdom the Jews wanted?

3. Why did Jesus avoid government issues?

4. Jesus didn't try to change the government even when it was dishonest and cruel. Does that mean that Christians should stay out of politics? Why or why not?

Mary Anoints Jesus   3

This study is based on Matthew 26:6–13; Mark 14:3–11;
Luke 7:36–50; John 11:55–57; 12:1–11;
and *The Desire of Ages,* chapter 62
—see also *Messiah,* chapter 62.

A feast at Simon's house

One of the few Pharisees who was a known follower of Jesus was Simon from the town of Bethany. Jesus had healed Simon of leprosy, and to show his gratitude, Simon threw a big party for Jesus and His disciples. Simon knew Jesus was a Healer and hoped that He might be the Messiah. But he didn't think of Jesus as his Savior or as the Son of God.

As He usually did, Jesus was staying at the home of His friends Mary, Martha, and Lazarus while He was in Bethany. Because Jesus was in town, crowds were everywhere. Many wanted to see the man Jesus had raised from the dead. Others thought Jesus would be crowned king during Passover.

The crowds weren't the only ones keeping an eye on Jesus. The priests and leaders were watching for a chance to do away with Him. But they feared Jesus would not attend Passover and would escape them.

With the story of the raising of Lazarus spreading like wildfire through the crowds, Jesus had become wildly popular with the people. The Sanhedrin—the Jewish court of religious leaders—met again to discuss what to do. "It would be dangerous to try to arrest Jesus publicly," one of the leaders said. "The crowds might turn on us."

"We must arrest him secretly," another agreed, "and keep the trial as quiet as possible."

The others nodded in agreement. "Once he's condemned to die, the people will begin to doubt him quickly enough."

"Lazarus will have to die as well," they agreed. "As long as he's alive, the people will remember Jesus' power." They feared that the people might even plan revenge on their leaders for taking the life of someone who could perform that kind of miracle.

While this plotting was going on, Jesus and His friends were attending Simon's dinner. Simon sat on one side of Jesus while Lazarus sat on the other. As usual, Martha helped serve the meal, while Mary stood nearby, listening to every word Jesus said.

Jesus had just done something extraordinary for Mary. He had forgiven her sins and had brought her brother back from death, and she wanted to do something to show her gratitude. Mary had heard Jesus say that He would soon die, and in her love and sorrow, she bought a very expensive alabaster jar of fragrant lotion to prepare His body for burial.

Reflect on the story

"Now many were declaring that He was about to be crowned king. Her grief was turned to joy, and she was eager to be first in honoring her Lord. Breaking her box of ointment, she poured its contents upon the head and feet of Jesus; then, as she knelt weeping, moistening them with her tears, she wiped His feet with her long, flowing hair.

"She had sought to avoid observation, and her movements might have passed unnoticed, but the ointment filled the room with its fragrance, and published her act to all present. Judas looked upon this act with great displeasure. Instead of waiting to hear what Christ would say of the matter, he began to whisper his complaints to those near him, throwing reproach upon Christ for suffering such waste. Craftily he made suggestions that would be likely to cause disaffection.

". . . Turning to the disciples, he asked, 'Why was not this ointment sold for three hundred pence, and given to the poor? This he said, not that he cared for the poor; but because he was a thief, and had the bag, and bare what was put therein.' Judas had no heart for the poor. Had Mary's ointment been sold, and the proceeds fallen into his possession, the poor would have received no benefit.

"Judas had a high opinion of his own executive ability. As a financier he thought himself greatly superior to his fellow disciples, and he had led them to regard him in the same light. He had gained their confidence, and had a strong influence over them. His professed sympathy for the poor deceived them, and his artful insinuation caused them to look distrustfully upon Mary's devotion. The murmur passed round the table, 'To what purpose is this waste? For this ointment might have been sold for much, and given to the poor.'

"Mary heard the words of criticism. Her heart trembled within her. She feared that her sister would reproach her for extravagance. The Master, too, might think her improvident. Without apology or excuse she was about to shrink away, when the voice of her Lord was heard, 'Let her alone; why trouble ye her?' He saw that she was embarrassed and distressed. He knew that in this act of service she had expressed her gratitude for the forgiveness of her sins, and He brought relief to her mind. Lifting His voice above the murmur of criticism, He said, 'She hath wrought a good work on Me. For ye have the poor with you always, and whensoever ye will ye may do them good: but Me ye have not always. She hath done what she could: she is come aforehand to anoint My body to the burying.'

"The fragrant gift which Mary had thought to lavish upon the dead body of the Saviour she poured upon His living form. At the burial its sweetness could only have pervaded the tomb; now it gladdened His heart with the assurance of her faith and love. Joseph of Arimathaea and Nicodemus offered not their gift of love to Jesus in His life. With bitter tears they brought their costly spices for His cold, unconscious form. The women who bore spices to the tomb found their errand in vain, for He had risen. But Mary, pouring out her love upon the Saviour while He was conscious of her devotion, was anointing Him for the burial. And as He went down into the darkness of His great trial, He carried with Him the memory of that deed, an earnest of the love that would be His from His redeemed ones forever.

"Many there are who bring their precious gifts for the dead. As they stand about the cold, silent form, words of love are freely spoken. Tenderness, appreciation, devotion, all are lavished upon one who sees not nor hears. Had these words been spoken when the weary spirit needed them so much, when the ear could hear and the heart could feel, how precious would have been their fragrance! . . .

"Christ told Mary the meaning of her act, and in this He gave her more than He had received. 'In that she hath poured this ointment on My body,' He said, 'she did it for My burial.' As the alabaster box was broken, and filled the whole house with its fragrance, so Christ was to die, His body was to be broken; but He was to rise from the tomb, and the fragrance of His life was to fill the earth. Christ 'hath loved us, and hath given Himself for us an offering and a sacrifice to God for a sweet-smelling savor.' Ephesians 5:2.

" 'Verily I say unto you,' Christ declared, 'Wheresoever this gospel shall be preached throughout the whole world, this also that she hath done shall be spoken of for a memorial of her.' Looking into the future, the Saviour spoke with certainty concerning His gospel. It was to be preached throughout the world. And as far as the gospel extended, Mary's gift would shed its fragrance, and hearts would be blessed through her unstudied act. Kingdoms would rise and fall; the names of monarchs and conquerors would be forgotten; but this woman's deed would be immortalized upon the pages of sacred history. Until time should be no more, that broken alabaster box would tell the story of the abundant love of God for a fallen race. . . .

"The disciples were not like Judas. They loved the Saviour. But they did not rightly appreciate His exalted character. Had they realized what He had done for them, they would have felt that nothing bestowed upon Him was wasted. The wise men from the East, who knew so little of Jesus, had shown a truer appreciation of the honor due Him. They brought precious gifts to the Saviour, and bowed in homage before Him when He was but a babe, and cradled in a manger. . . .

"Christ delighted in the earnest desire of Mary to do the will of her Lord. He accepted the wealth of pure affection which His disciples did not, would not, understand. The desire that Mary had to do this service for her Lord was of more value to Christ than all the precious ointment in the world, because it expressed her appreciation of the world's Redeemer. It was the love of Christ that constrained her. The matchless excellence of the character of Christ filled her soul. That ointment was a symbol of the heart of the giver. It was the outward demonstration of a love fed by heavenly streams until it overflowed.

"The work of Mary was just the lesson the disciples needed to show them that the expression of their love for Him would be pleasing to Christ. He had been everything to them, and they did not realize that soon they would be deprived of His presence, that soon they could offer Him no token of their gratitude for His great love. The loneliness of Christ, separated from the heavenly courts, living the life of humanity, was never understood or appreciated by the disciples as it should have been. He was often grieved because His disciples did not give Him that which He should have received from them. He knew that if they were under the influence of the heavenly angels that accompanied Him, they too would think no offering of sufficient value to declare the heart's spiritual affection.

"Their afterknowledge gave them a true sense of the many things they might have done for Jesus expressive of the love and gratitude of their hearts, while they were near Him. When Jesus was no longer with them, and they felt indeed as sheep without a shepherd, they began to see how they might have shown Him attentions that would have brought gladness to His heart. They no longer cast blame upon Mary, but upon themselves. Oh, if they could have taken back their censuring, their presenting the poor as more worthy of the gift than was Christ! They felt the reproof keenly as they took from the cross the bruised body of their Lord.

"The same want is evident in our world today. But few appreciate all that Christ is to them. If they did, the great love of Mary would be expressed, the anointing would be freely bestowed. The expensive ointment would not be called a waste. Nothing would be thought too costly to give for Christ, no self-denial or self-sacrifice too great to be endured for His sake" (*The Desire of Ages,* 559–565; see also *Messiah,* 306–308).

Questions to consider

1. What did Judas criticize about Mary's gift? Was it selfish of Jesus to say, "The poor will always be with you, but I won't"? Why not?

2. What does this story tell us about the value of gifts honoring the dead?

3. Mary's story has been told and retold many times. What has it taught you?

Reflect on the story

"Simon was surprised at Jesus' reaction to Mary. He thought to himself, 'If he was really a prophet, he would have known that a sinful woman was touching him.' But Simon didn't know what God and Jesus are really like—kind and merciful. Simon thought that sinners should be pointed out and avoided.

"Jesus knew what Simon was thinking. He said, 'Simon, I have a story for you. A certain man had two debtors. One owed 500 pence and the other 50 pence. When neither of them could pay the money back, he forgave them both. So tell me, which one of them will love him the most?'

"Simon replied, 'I suppose the one that was forgiven the most.'

"Jesus said, 'You are right.' Using a story as the prophet Nathan had done with King David, Jesus let Simon condemn himself. Simon had led Mary into sin. She had been deeply mistreated by him. The two debtors in the story represented Simon and Mary. Jesus wasn't teaching that they owed different debts of gratitude to God. They each owed more than could be repaid. Jesus wanted to show Simon that his sin was as much greater than Mary's as a 500-pence debt is greater than a 50-pence debt.

"Simon began to see himself differently. As shame seized him, he realized that he was in the presence of Someone greater than any human.

"Jesus went on. 'When I came into your house, you gave Me no water to wash My feet. You did not greet Me with a kiss, but this woman has kissed my feet over and over.' Then He responded to what Simon had been thinking. 'See this woman? Her many sins are forgiven, so she loves very much. Someone who is forgiven for only a few sins loves only a little.'

"Simon thought He was honoring Jesus with a dinner. Now he saw that he was not honoring Him at all. He saw that his own religion was a farce, and that while Mary was a sinner, she was forgiven. Simon was a sinner, but was not forgiven.

"Simon was touched by Jesus' kindness in not exposing his sins to the others. He had not been treated as he wanted Mary to be treated. A stern rebuke would have hardened him against repenting, but Jesus was trying to win his heart by love. As he finally understood his great debt, he confessed his sins. The proud Pharisee became a humble follower.

"Jesus knew what had happened to shape Mary's life. He could have destroyed her last hopes, but He didn't. He lifted her up, casting demons out of her seven times. When others saw her as a hopeless case, Jesus saw the good in her. By His grace, she became a different person. Mary sat at His feet and listened. Mary spread lotion on His head and washed His feet with her tears. Mary stood beside the cross and followed His body to the tomb. Mary was the first to announce that He had risen.

"Jesus knows all about every person. You may think you are very sinful, but the worse you are, the more you need Jesus. He won't turn any sincerely sorrowful person away. He freely pardons all who come to Him for forgiveness and bonds them to His own divine-human nature where no human or evil angel can tear them away. They stand beside Him, the great Sin Bearer, in the light from the throne of God. He died to take the blame and the pain for their sins" (*Messiah*, 309, 310; see also *The Desire of Ages*, 566–568).

Questions to consider

1. How did Jesus help Simon understand forgiveness? What can we learn about forgiving others?

2. The worse the things are that you've done, the more you need Jesus. What does Jesus' repeated forgiveness of Mary say to you?

"Hosanna to the King!"   4

This study is based on Matthew 21:1–11; Mark 11:1–10;
Luke 19:29–44; John 12:12–19; and *The Desire of Ages,* chapter 63
—see also *Messiah,* chapter 63.

Riding on a donkey

The day dawned bright and glorious. The green of the trees formed a glowing backdrop to the growing bouquet of spring flowers. On a day when even nature seemed to be rejoicing, there was great hope for a new kingdom. Passover was about to begin, and the people who had crowded into the small town of Bethany to see Jesus now began to make their way toward Jerusalem.

Deciding to ride into Jerusalem, Jesus directed two disciples where to find the animal on which He would ride. "Go there and you will find a donkey's colt tied up. Untie it and bring it to Me. If anyone asks why you are taking the colt, say that the Master needs it."

And so they did, returning quickly with the donkey. The disciples were amazed that Jesus wanted to go to Jerusalem and astounded that He wanted to ride a donkey. He had never ridden anywhere before! But it gave them hope that He was finally ready to enter the capital city and proclaim Himself King.

Five hundred years before Jesus was born, the prophet Zechariah had foretold the day a king would come to Israel: "Rejoice greatly, people of Jerusalem! Shout for joy, people of Jerusalem! Your king is coming to you. He does what is right, and he saves. He is gentle and riding on a donkey, on the colt of a donkey" (Zechariah 9:9, NCV).

Jesus was simply following the Jewish custom for a royal visit. And the people along the road immediately recognized the significance. As soon as Jesus was seated on the donkey, the shouting began. "Hail the Messiah! Hail the King! Blessed is He who comes in the name of the Lord!" Imagining the Romans driven from their city and Israel once more a powerful nation, each person tried to outshout the others. They competed to honor Jesus, but since they had no gifts, people spread their coats to carpet the path in front of Him. Others cut palm and olive tree branches and laid them along the road. With no royal banners to wave, they cut palm branches and waved them over their heads.

As the crowd swelled to line the road, other travelers rushed up to ask, "Who is this? What does it mean?"

When the priests at the temple blew the trumpet to summon worshipers to the evening service, only a few people responded. "The whole world must be following Jesus," the priests and rulers said to one another.

Reflect on the story

"Never before in His earthly life had Jesus permitted such a demonstration. He clearly foreraw the result. It would bring Him to the cross. But it was His purpose thus publicly to present Himself as the Redeemer. He desired to call attention to the sacrifice that was to crown His mission to a fallen world. While the people were assembling at Jerusalem to celebrate the Passover, He, the antitypical Lamb, by a voluntary act set Himself apart as an oblation. It would be needful for His church in all succeeding ages to make His death for the sins of the world a subject of deep thought and study. Every fact connected with it should be verified beyond a doubt. It was necessary, then, that the eyes of all people should now be directed to Him; the events which preceded His great sacrifice must be such as to call attention to the sacrifice itself. After such a demonstration as that attending His entry into Jerusalem, all eyes would follow His rapid progress to the final scene.

"The events connected with this triumphal ride would be the talk of every tongue, and would bring Jesus before every mind. After His crucifixion, many would recall these events in their connection with His trial and death. They would be led to search the prophecies, and would be convinced that Jesus was the Messiah; and in all lands converts to the faith would be multiplied.

"In this one triumphant scene of His earthly life, the Saviour might have appeared escorted by heavenly angels, and heralded by the trump of God; but such a demonstration would have been contrary to the purpose of His mission, contrary to the law which had governed His life. He remained true to the humble lot He had accepted. The burden of humanity He must bear until His life was given for the life of the world.

"This day, which seemed to the disciples the crowning day of their lives, would have been shadowed with gloomy clouds had they known that this scene of rejoicing was but a prelude to the suffering and death of their Master. Although He had repeatedly told them of His certain sacrifice, yet in the glad triumph of the present they forgot His sorrowful words, and looked forward to His prosperous reign on David's throne.

"New accessions were made continually to the procession, and, with few exceptions, all who joined it caught the inspiration of the hour, and helped to swell the hosannas that echoed and re-echoed from hill to hill and from valley to valley. The shouts went up continually, 'Hosanna to the Son of David: Blessed is He that cometh in the name of the Lord! Hosanna in the highest.'

"Never before had the world seen such a triumphal procession. It was not like that of the earth's famous conquerors. No train of mourning captives, as trophies of kingly valor, made a feature of that scene. But about the Saviour were the glorious trophies of His labors of love for sinful man. There were the captives whom He had rescued from Satan's power, praising God for their deliverance. The blind whom He had restored to sight were leading the way. The dumb whose tongues He had loosed shouted the loudest hosannas. The cripples whom He had healed bounded with joy, and were the most active in breaking the palm branches and waving them before the Saviour. Widows and orphans were exalting the name of Jesus for His works of mercy to them. The lepers whom He had cleansed spread their untainted garments in His path, and hailed Him as the King of glory. Those whom His voice had awakened from the sleep of death were in that throng. Lazarus, whose body had seen corruption in the grave, but who now rejoiced in the strength of glorious manhood, led the beast on which the Saviour rode.

"Many Pharisees witnessed the scene, and, burning with envy and malice, sought to turn the current of popular feeling. With all their authority they tried to silence the people; but their appeals and threats only increased the enthusiasm. They feared that this multitude, in the strength of their numbers, would make Jesus king. As a last resort they pressed through the crowd to where the Saviour was, and accosted Him with reproving and threatening words: 'Master, rebuke Thy disciples.' They declared that such noisy demonstrations were unlawful, and would not be permitted by the authorities. But they were silenced by the reply of Jesus, 'I tell you that, if these should hold their peace, the stones would immediately cry out.' That scene of triumph was of God's own appointing. It had been foretold by the prophet, and man was powerless to turn aside God's purpose. Had men failed to carry out His plan, He would have given a voice to the inanimate stones, and they would have hailed His Son with acclamations of praise. As the silenced Pharisees drew back, the words of Zechariah were taken up by hundreds of voices: 'Rejoice greatly, O daughter of Zion; shout, O daughter of Jerusalem: behold, thy King cometh unto thee: He is just, and having salvation; lowly, and riding upon an ass, and upon a colt the foal of an ass.'

"When the procession reached the brow of the hill, and was about to descend into the city, Jesus halted, and all the multitude with Him. Before them lay Jerusalem in its glory, now bathed in the light of the declining sun. The temple attracted all eyes. In stately grandeur it towered above all else, seeming to point toward heaven as if directing the people to the only true and living God. The temple had long been the pride and glory of the Jewish nation. The Romans also prided themselves in its magnificence. A king appointed by the Romans had united with the Jews to rebuild and embellish it, and the emperor of Rome had enriched it with his gifts. Its strength, richness, and magnificence had made it one of the wonders of the world" (*The Desire of Ages,* 571–575; see also *Messiah,* 312, 313).

Questions to consider

1. Why did Jesus allow this royal procession? What price would He pay for it?

2. How did this procession compare to those of the world's great conquerors? What "trophies" went before Jesus?

Reflect on the story

"The crowd was spellbound by this vision of beauty. But when they turned to watch Jesus' reaction to the sight, they were shocked to see tears in His eyes. With a cry of grief, Jesus rocked back and forth like a tree in a windstorm. What a sight for the angels to see! What a sight for the excited crowd that thought they were escorting Him to His throne! Israel's king was in tears of agony. A cloud of sadness covered the whole crowd. Many of the people cried with Jesus without understanding why.

"From where He was, Jesus could see Gethsemane, where He would face the darkest hours of His life. Nearby was Calvary where He would suffer and die. Just in front of Him was the sheep gate, through which sheep for the sacrifices had been led for hundreds of years. But these things didn't cause Jesus' sorrow. It was the sight of Jerusalem that broke His heart—the city that had rejected the Son of God and was about to take His life. He saw what Jerusalem could have been—how could He give up on her?

"God had favored the people of Israel. Their temple had been His home on earth. But all the symbols and ceremonies must now end. Jesus reached out toward the city and said, ' "I wish you knew today what would bring you peace. But now it is hidden from you" ' (Luke 19:42, NCV). What Jesus didn't say was what could have happened if Jerusalem had accepted God's Gift. She could have been free and prosperous, a mighty city, the world's crown of peace and glory.

"But Jesus knew that the city was doomed. He saw the time when enemies would surround the city and the people would starve and die. He saw crosses standing as thick as forests on Calvary. He saw the palaces destroyed, the temple demolished, the very stones of the walls scattered, and the ground left plowed like a garden. He said, ' "All this will happen because you did not recognize the time when God came to save you" ' (Luke 19:44, NCV).

"But God's Holy Spirit would speak to Jerusalem one more time. Before the day ended, Jesus would appeal to her again. If He was accepted, Jerusalem might still be saved!

"But the city's leaders had no welcome for the Son of God. As the procession started down the hill, they demanded to know, 'Who is this?'

"The disciples, inspired by the Holy Spirit, repeated all the prophecies pointing to Jesus. Then they declared their own testimony: 'This is Jesus, the Messiah, the Prince of life, the Savior of the world' " (*Messiah*, 313, 314; see also *The Desire of Ages*, 575–579).

Questions to consider

1. What would have happened if Jerusalem had accepted Jesus?

2. Jesus wept because Jerusalem and His people had rejected Him. Has your church every given Him reason to weep? Has your home?

The Last Supper   5

This study is based on Matthew 26:20–29; Mark 14:17–25;
Luke 22:7–24; John 13:1–30; and *The Desire of Ages,* chapters 71, 72
—see also *Messiah,* chapters 71, 72.

Servant of servants

As they entered upper room that evening for the Passover meal, the disciples had returned to their argument about who would have the most powerful position in Jesus' kingdom. James and John's bold request for these positions still angered the others, especially Judas. Judas pushed his way to the seat on the left side of Jesus at the table. John had taken the right side. Whatever the most important office would be in the new kingdom, Judas was determined to have it.

On this last evening, Jesus had much to tell them. But as He looked into their eyes, He said nothing. They weren't ready to hear what He had to say. As the silent moments passed, they pretended to be unaware that they were ignoring a duty that disciples should perform.

Unlike the da Vinci painting we all know, the Passover supper that evening would have been eaten as the guests lay on couches placed around a low table. The guests' heads were close to the table, while their feet could be washed by someone passing around the outside of the circle.

The custom at a meal like this was for a servant to come in and wash the feet of the guests. A pitcher of water, a washing basin, and towel had all been provided with the room, but no servant was available. With their Teacher present, one of the disciples should have offered to serve. But none of them was willing to be seen as a servant.

For a time, Jesus waited to see what they would do. Then He stood, took off His cloak, and picked up the towel. Shocked and ashamed, the disciples stared as He began to wash their feet. They realized how they had been behaving. The example Jesus gave was a lesson they would never forget. His love for them was so strong that He was willing to lay aside His royal dignity and take the role of servant.

Jesus knew that Judas had already agreed to betray Him, but He washed his feet anyway. The love Jesus' actions revealed tempted Judas to repent, but his pride was too strong. He hardened his heart and convinced himself that no true king would humble himself as Jesus was doing. He determined to go ahead with his plan of betrayal.

By washing their feet—even Peter's, in spite of his shamed objection—Jesus had changed their hearts. Except for Judas, each one was ready for someone else to have the most important position. Now they were ready to listen and learn.

Reflect on the story

"After Christ had washed the disciples' feet, and had taken His garments and sat down

29

again, He said to them, 'Know ye what I have done to you?' . . .

"Christ would have His disciples understand that although He had washed their feet, this did not in the least detract from His dignity. 'Ye call Me Master and Lord: and ye say well; for so I am.' And being so infinitely superior, He imparted grace and significance to the service. No one was so exalted as Christ, and yet He stooped to the humblest duty. That His people might not be misled by the selfishness which dwells in the natural heart, and which strengthens by self-serving, Christ Himself set the example of humility. He would not leave this great subject in man's charge. Of so much consequence did He regard it, that He Himself, One equal with God, acted as servant to His disciples. While they were contending for the highest place, He to whom every knee shall bow, He whom the angels of glory count it honor to serve, bowed down to wash the feet of those who called Him Lord. He washed the feet of His betrayer.

"In His life and lessons, Christ has given a perfect exemplification of the unselfish ministry which has its origin in God. God does not live for Himself. By creating the world, and by upholding all things, He is constantly ministering for others. 'He maketh His sun to rise on the evil and on the good, and sendeth rain on the just and on the unjust.' Matthew 5:45. This ideal of ministry God has committed to His Son. Jesus was given to stand at the head of humanity, that by His example He might teach what it means to minister. His whole life was under a law of service. He served all, ministered to all. Thus He lived the law of God, and by His example showed how we are to obey it.

"Again and again Jesus had tried to establish this principle among His disciples. When James and John made their request for pre-eminence, He had said, 'Whosoever will be great among you, let him be your minister.' Matthew 20:26. In My kingdom the principle of preference and supremacy has no place. The only greatness is the greatness of humility. The only distinction is found in devotion to the service of others.

"Now, having washed the disciples' feet, He said, 'I have given you an example, that ye should do as I have done to you.' In these words Christ was not merely enjoining the practice of hospitality. More was meant than the washing of the feet of guests to remove the dust of travel. Christ was here instituting a religious service. By the act of our Lord this humiliating ceremony was made a consecrated ordinance. It was to be observed by the disciples, that they might ever keep in mind His lessons of humility and service.

"This ordinance is Christ's appointed preparation for the sacramental service. While pride, variance, and strife for supremacy are cherished, the heart cannot enter into fellowship with Christ. We are not prepared to receive the communion of His body and His blood. Therefore it was that Jesus appointed the memorial of His humiliation to be first observed.

". . . There is in man a disposition to esteem himself more highly than his brother, to work for self, to seek the highest place; and often this results in evil surmisings and bitterness of spirit. The ordinance preceding the Lord's Supper is to clear away these misunderstandings, to bring man out of his selfishness, down from his stilts of self-exaltation, to the humility of heart that will lead him to serve his brother. . . .

"As the lesson of the preparatory service is thus learned, the desire is kindled for a higher spiritual life. To this desire the divine Witness will respond. The soul will be uplifted. We can partake of the Communion with a consciousness of sins forgiven. The sunshine of Christ's righteousness will fill the chambers of the mind and the soul temple. We 'behold the Lamb of God, which taketh away the sin of the world.' John 1:29.

"To those who receive the spirit of this service, it can never become a mere ceremonial. Its constant lesson will be, 'By love serve one another.' Galatians 5:13. In washing the feet of His disciples, Christ gave evidence that He would do any service, however humble, that would make them heirs with Him of the eternal wealth of heaven's treasure. His disciples, in performing the same rite, pledge themselves in like manner to serve their brethren. Whenever this ordinance is rightly celebrated, the children of God are brought into a holy relationship, to help and bless each other. They covenant that the life shall be given to unselfish ministry. . . .

"Jesus, the served of all, came to be the servant of all. And because He ministered to all, He will again be served and honored by all. And those who would partake of His divine attributes, and share with Him the joy of seeing souls redeemed, must follow His example of unselfish ministry.

"All this was comprehended in the words of Jesus, 'I have given you an example, that ye should do as I have done to you.' This was the intent of the service He established. And He says, 'If ye know these things,' if you know the purpose of His lessons, 'happy are ye if ye do them' " (*The Desire of Ages*, 649–651; see also *Messiah, 349, 350*).

Questions to consider

1. "God does not live for Himself." How do we live for others as God does?

2. What does the foot-washing ordinance help clear away in each of us?

3. What memories does a foot-washing service bring to your mind? How could you make it more like the experience the disciples had?

Reflect on the story

"When believers gather for the Lord's Supper, it is not a time to focus on their shortcomings or on the differences between them. The foot-washing ceremony dealt with those issues. Now they are meeting with Jesus, not in the shadow of the Cross, but in its saving light. They can open their souls to the bright beams of Jesus, the Sun of Righteousness.

"At these services the Lord speaks to us saying, 'If you feel oppressed or distressed because of Me or the gospel, remember that My love is so strong that I gave My life for you. When your work is too hard or your burdens are too heavy, remember that I suffered the shame of the cross for you. And I now live to stand and speak for you in heaven.'

"The Communion service was designed to keep the hope of Jesus' second coming alive in our minds. 'Every time you eat this bread and drink this cup you are telling others about the Lord's death until he comes' (1 Corinthians 11:26, NCV).

A Thoughtful Hour

"This service reminds us of God's love. It reminds us that Jesus' death on the cross created a permanent connection between God and humans. It can help us understand what Jesus suffered to pay for our sins and save us. It reminds us that because of Jesus' death, we can look forward to His second coming with real joy.

"Jesus' death allows humans to live on, filled with hope. We owe even our everyday lives to His sacrifice. The cross of Calvary is stamped on every loaf of bread and reflected in every well of water. His blood paid for our bread and water.

"Eating Jesus' body and drinking His blood means accepting His words and doing the things He commands us to do. Jesus lived by His Father's will; when we accept Jesus, we live by His will. Every Communion service forms a living connection from us to Jesus and by Him to the Father.

"When we share the bread and wine that represents Jesus' broken body and spilled blood, we can in our imagination relive the sacrifice He made. The thought of what happened on Calvary will create holy emotions—selfless love—in our hearts. Pride and self-centeredness cannot exist in a heart that remembers the Cross. Any person who sees the Savior's matchless love will be changed. That person will go out to be a light to the world, a reflection of that mysterious love" (*Messiah*, 354, 355; see also *The Desire of Ages*, 659–661).

Questions to consider

1. What does the Lord say to us through the Communion service? What does this service remind us of?

2. What aspects of the Communion service speak most clearly to you? How do they inspire you to accept Jesus' words and follow His way?

3. Does celebrating the Lord's Supper affect your life? Can you remember a service that touched you in a special way?

Knowing the Way 6

This study is based on John 13:31–38; 14–17;
and *The Desire of Ages,* chapter 73
—see also *Messiah,* chapter 73.

The way to heaven

Now that Judas had left the group, Jesus wanted to prepare the other disciples for what was coming. When He said, "I will be with you only a little longer," they were troubled and worried. But Jesus' next words reassured them.

Jesus said, "Don't let your hearts be troubled. . . . I am going there [my Father's house] to prepare a place for you. After I go and prepare a place for you, I will come back and take you to be with me so that you may be where I am. You know the way to the place where I am going" (John 14:1–4, NCV).

Thomas was still worried. "Lord, we don't know where You are going. How can we know the way?" Maybe Thomas was asking for a map or some specific directions, but Jesus' answer went much deeper.

"I am the way."

We may feel that we understand Jesus better than His disciples did. But how often do we have the same question? How can we know the right way to follow Jesus? How can we be sure that we're living the right way to get to heaven?

The answer to our questions is the same as Jesus' response to Thomas: "I am the way."

When the Christian life seems complicated and overwhelming, Jesus' answer to His disciples' question is the answer we need as well. "I am the way," He said. "Walk in My footsteps. Follow Me. When you know Me, you know My Father. And because you do know Me, you know what My Father in heaven is like."

The disciples claimed to believe that Jesus was the Son of God, but they still had trouble understanding what that relationship meant. It was Philip who said the words out loud. "Lord, show us the Father. That's all we need. Then we won't worry."

Imagine seeing Jesus' head bow and His shoulders slump just a little before He answers. "I've been with you a long time now, Philip. Do you still not know Me? If you have seen Me, you have seen the Father. Why are you asking this? Don't you believe that the Father is in Me? The things I've been saying to you don't come from Me, but from My Father."

If the disciples had understood that connection, they wouldn't have lost their faith when Jesus' died. Even when they didn't understand what was happening, they would have been able to trust the Father.

Reflect on the story

"Before offering Himself as the sacrificial victim, Christ sought for the most essential and complete gift to bestow upon His followers, a gift that would bring within their reach the boundless resources of grace. 'I will pray to the Father,' He said, 'and He shall give you another Comforter, that He may abide with you forever; even the Spirit of truth; whom the world cannot receive, because it seeth Him not, neither knoweth Him: but ye know Him; for He dwelleth with you, and shall be in you. I will not leave you orphans: I will come to you.' John 14:16–18, margin.

"Before this the Spirit had been in the world; from the very beginning of the work of redemption He had been moving upon men's hearts. But while Christ was on earth, the disciples had desired no other helper. Not until they were deprived of His presence would they feel their need of the Spirit, and then He would come.

"The Holy Spirit is Christ's representative, but divested of the personality of humanity, and independent thereof. Cumbered with humanity, Christ could not be in every place personally. Therefore it was for their interest that He should go to the Father, and send the Spirit to be His successor on earth. No one could then have any advantage because of his location or his personal contact with Christ. By the Spirit the Saviour would be accessible to all. In this sense He would be nearer to them than if He had not ascended on high. . . .

"At all times and in all places, in all sorrows and in all afflictions, when the outlook seems dark and the future perplexing, and we feel helpless and alone, the Comforter will be sent in answer to the prayer of faith. Circumstances may separate us from every earthly friend; but no circumstance, no distance, can separate us from the heavenly Comforter. Wherever we are, wherever we may go, He is always at our right hand to support, sustain, uphold, and cheer. . . .

"The disciples were to bear witness to the life and work of Christ. Through their word He was to speak to all the people on the face of the earth. But in the humiliation and death of Christ they were to suffer great trial and disappointment. That after this experience their word might be accurate, Jesus promised that the Comforter should 'bring all things to your remembrance, whatsoever I have said unto you.'

". . . Jesus had opened before His disciples a vast tract of truth. But it was most difficult for them to keep His lessons distinct from the traditions and maxims of the scribes and Pharisees. They had been educated to accept the teaching of the rabbis as the voice of God, and it still held a power over their minds, and molded their sentiments. Earthly ideas, temporal things, still had a large place in their thoughts. They did not understand the spiritual nature of Christ's kingdom, though He had so often explained it to them. Their minds had become confused. They did not comprehend the value of the scriptures Christ presented. Many of His lessons seemed almost lost upon them. Jesus saw that they did not lay hold of the real meaning of His words. He compassionately promised that the Holy Spirit should recall these sayings to their minds. And He had left unsaid many things that could not be comprehended by the disciples. These also would be opened to them by the Spirit. The Spirit was to quicken their understanding, that they might have an appreciation of heavenly things. 'When He, the Spirit of truth, is come,' said Jesus, 'He will guide you into all truth.'

"The Comforter is called 'the Spirit of truth.' His work is to define and maintain the truth. He first dwells in the heart as the Spirit of truth, and thus He becomes the Comforter. There is comfort and peace in the truth, but no real peace or comfort can be found in falsehood. It is through false theories and traditions that Satan gains his power over the mind. By directing men to false standards, he misshapes the character. Through the Scriptures the Holy Spirit speaks to the mind, and impresses truth upon the heart. Thus He exposes error, and expels it from the soul. It is by the Spirit of truth, working through the word of God, that Christ subdues His chosen people to Himself. . . .

". . . The preaching of the word will be of no avail without the continual presence and aid of the Holy Spirit. This is the only effectual teacher of divine truth. Only when the truth is accompanied to the heart by the Spirit will it quicken the conscience or transform the life. One might be able to present the letter of the word of God, he might be familiar with all its commands and promises; but unless the Holy Spirit sets home the truth, no souls will fall on the Rock and be broken. No amount of education, no advantages, however great, can make one a channel of light without the co-operation of the Spirit of God. The sowing of the gospel seed will not be a success unless the seed is quickened into life by the dew of heaven. Before one book of the New Testament was written, before one gospel sermon had been preached after Christ's ascension, the Holy Spirit came upon the praying apostles. Then the testimony of their enemies was, 'Ye have filled Jerusalem with your doctrine.' Acts 5:28.

"Christ has promised the gift of the Holy Spirit to His church, and the promise belongs to us as much as to the first disciples. But like every other promise, it is given on conditions. There are many who believe and profess to claim the Lord's promise; they talk *about* Christ and *about* the Holy Spirit, yet receive no benefit. They do not surrender the soul to be guided and controlled by the divine agencies. We cannot use the Holy Spirit. The Spirit is to use us. Through the Spirit God works in His people 'to will and to do of His good pleasure.' Philippians 2:13. But many will not submit to this. They want to manage themselves. This is why they do not receive the heavenly gift. Only to those who wait humbly upon God, who watch for His guidance and grace, is the Spirit given. The power of God awaits their demand and reception. This promised blessing, claimed by faith, brings all other blessings in its train. It is given according to the riches of the grace of Christ, and He is ready to supply every soul according to the capacity to receive" (*The Desire of Ages*, 668–672; see also *Messiah*, 359, 360).

Questions to consider

1. Why is it an advantage to us that Jesus returned to heaven and that the Holy Spirit took His place on earth?

2. Why were the disciples able to understand so little of what Jesus taught them? What did Jesus do after He left to help them and to help us?

3. The Holy Spirit was given to us as much as to the disciples. Why do we receive so little benefit from it?

Reflect on the story

"As they walked toward the Garden of Gethsemane through the bright moonlight, Jesus noticed a grapevine and drew the disciples' attention to it. 'I am the True Vine,' He said, 'and My Father is the Gardener.' Unlike the strong palm and oak trees, the grapevine needs support to grow toward heaven. Like the vine, Jesus depended on His Father's power.

" 'I am the Vine,' Jesus said, 'and you are the branches.' Like branches that are grafted onto the vine, Jesus' followers must grow into a relationship with Him. Then like the branch, we will receive life through our connection to Him. Our weaknesses are united with His strengths. This is how we can have the mind of Jesus—how we can think and act like Jesus did.

"But this cannot be an on-again, off-again relationship. Jesus said, ' "Remain in me, and I will remain in you. A branch cannot produce fruit alone but must remain in the vine. In the same way, you cannot produce fruit alone but must remain in me" ' (John 15:4, NCV). Our relationship with Jesus must be constant—every moment of every day—in order to stay strong. Without Him, we cannot overcome temptations. We must hold on tight to Jesus, then by faith we can receive His perfect character.

"When we live by faith in Jesus, our lives will be changed—the fruits of the Spirit will be seen. Many act like Christians, and claim to be Christians, but their characters will show if they have any real connection to Jesus. If they produce no fruit—no kindness or love for others—they are false branches. Branches that produce no fruit are cut off and burned.

"Branches that produce fruit are pruned—trimmed so that they can produce even more and better fruit. Of the twelve disciples, one was a false branch about to be cut off, and the others were soon to be pruned by a terrible ordeal. Pruning can be painful, but it's our Father the Gardener who does the pruning. He works to make us stronger, wiser, better followers of Jesus.

". . . But Jesus didn't teach His disciples to work hard to bear this fruit. He told them to remain in Him, to keep their connection to Him. Living in Jesus, following Jesus, supported by Jesus, we will produce fruit like His.

"Jesus' first words when He was alone with His disciples in the upper room that night was: ' "I give you a new command: Love each other. You must love each other as I have loved you" ' (John 13:34, NCV). To the disciples, this was new. They had not had much love for each other. But they were developing a new understanding of love. This command to love each other had a new meaning after they witnessed Jesus' sacrifice.

"When people take care of each other—not because they are forced to or because of some personal benefit—they are showing the influence of heaven. It is evidence that the image of God is being re-created in humans. And this kind of love in the church will stir Satan's anger. Jesus told His disciples, 'If the world hates you, remember that it hated Me first. If they did wrong to Me, they will do wrong to you too.' Showing the kind of love Jesus did will get the same response from those controlled by Satan—hate.

"As the Savior of the world, most of the time Jesus didn't seem to have much success. He was not able to do much of the work He wanted to do. Satan and those he influenced were always working against Him. But He would be not discouraged. He knew that when He cried out, 'It is finished,' all heaven would claim victory. He knew that His triumph would be trumpeted from world to world throughout the universe. He knew that truth—armed with the power of the Holy Spirit—would win the battle with evil.

"He knew that His disciples' lives would be like His—a string of successful battles that might not seem like victories when they happened. But in eternity, they would be recognized as the triumphs they really were.

"We should live as Jesus lived, work as He worked, and have the same faithful endurance that He had. Instead of being discouraged with difficulties, we can overcome the problems we face" (*Messiah*, 362–364; see also *The Desire of Ages*, 674–679).

Questions to consider

1. Why did Jesus describe us as a grapevine rather than as a palm tree or oak? How does being weak like grapevines help us bear better fruit?

2. How can we be certain we have a real connection to Jesus?

3. What is revealed when people take care of one another? Do you see it in your church? In yourself?

4. By human standards, Jesus' work while He was on earth was mostly unsuccessful. How can that encourage us?

The Struggle in Gethsemane   7

This study is based on Matthew 26:36–56; Mark 14:32–50;
Luke 22:39–53; John 18:1–12; and *The Desire of Ages,* chapter 74
—see also *Messiah,* chapter 74.

"Let this cup pass from Me"

At the foot of the Mount of Olives, just outside the city of Jerusalem, stood the Garden of Gethsemane. This quiet grove of olive trees was quite familiar to Jesus and His disciples. They often rested and slept there while visiting the city.

With their Passover meal behind them and some of the most beautiful teachings of Jesus fresh in their ears, the disciples followed Jesus through the bright moonlight. As the neared the garden, Jesus grew quiet. This night was different, and He could feel it.

Every day of His life on earth, Jesus had lived in the light of God's presence. But now the time was approaching when that light would be removed, when He would be counted as a sinner, guilty of the sin of fallen humans. That guilt was so heavy that Jesus was tempted to fear that it would separate Him eternally from His Father's love. He cried out, "My heart is full of sorrow, to the point of death."

"Please wait here and pray," Jesus said to eight of the disciples as they entered the Garden. "Peter, James, John, please come with Me."

They went some distance farther before John whispered to James, "I've never seen Him so sad. Help me find His usual resting spot." Before they reached it, Jesus would have fallen twice if they hadn't supported Him.

These three disciples had often prayed with Him in this garden. They would pray for a time, then sleep until Jesus woke them in the morning. Now He requested them to spend the night in prayer with Him.

But on this night, Jesus didn't want them to witness His great struggle. He left the three disciples and went a little distance farther. There He fell to the ground. He could feel that sin was separating Him from His Father. And that separation seemed so wide and so deep that His heart shuddered to think of it. He chose not to use His divine power to escape it. As a human, Jesus had to suffer the results of human sin. As a human, He had to endure God's anger at sin.

Reflect on the story

"Christ was now standing in a different attitude from that in which He had ever stood before. His suffering can best be described in the words of the prophet, 'Awake, O sword, against My shepherd, and against the man that is My fellow, saith the Lord of hosts.' Zechariah 13:7. As the substitute and surety for sinful man, Christ was suffering under divine justice. He saw what justice meant. Hitherto He had been as an intercessor for others; now He longed to have an intercessor for Himself.

"As Christ felt His unity with the Father broken up, He feared that in His human nature He would be unable to endure the coming conflict with the powers of darkness. In the wilderness of temptation the destiny of the human race had been at stake. Christ was then conqueror. Now the tempter had come for the last fearful struggle. For this he had been preparing during the three years of Christ's ministry. Everything was at stake with him. If he failed here, his hope of mastery was lost; the kingdoms of the world would finally become Christ's; he himself would be overthrown and cast out. But if Christ could be overcome, the earth would become Satan's kingdom, and the human race would be forever in his power. With the issues of the conflict before Him, Christ's soul was filled with dread of separation from God. Satan told Him that if He became the surety for a sinful world, the separation would be eternal. He would be identified with Satan's kingdom, and would nevermore be one with God.

"And what was to be gained by this sacrifice? How hopeless appeared the guilt and ingratitude of men! In its hardest features Satan pressed the situation upon the Redeemer: The people who claim to be above all others in temporal and spiritual advantages have rejected You. They are seeking to destroy You, the foundation, the center and seal of the promises made to them as a peculiar people. One of Your own disciples, who has listened to Your instruction, and has been among the foremost in church activities, will betray You. One of Your most zealous followers will deny You. All will forsake You. Christ's whole being abhorred the thought. That those whom He had undertaken to save, those whom He loved so much, should unite in the plots of Satan, this pierced His soul. . . .

"Behold Him contemplating the price to be paid for the human soul. In His agony He clings to the cold ground, as if to prevent Himself from being drawn farther from God. The chilling dew of night falls upon His prostrate form, but He heeds it not. From His pale lips comes the bitter cry, 'O My Father, if it be possible, let this cup pass from Me.' Yet even now He adds, 'Nevertheless not as I will, but as Thou wilt.'

"The human heart longs for sympathy in suffering. This longing Christ felt to the very depths of His being. In the supreme agony of His soul He came to His disciples with a yearning desire to hear some words of comfort from those whom He had so often blessed and comforted, and shielded in sorrow and distress. The One who had always had words of sympathy for them was now suffering superhuman agony, and He longed to know that they were praying for Him and for themselves. How dark seemed the malignity of sin! Terrible was the temptation to let the human race bear the consequences of its own guilt, while He stood innocent before God. If He could only know that His disciples understood and appreciated this, He would be strengthened.

"Rising with painful effort, He staggered to the place where He had left His companions. But He 'findeth them asleep.' Had He found them praying, He would have been relieved. Had they been seeking refuge in God, that satanic agencies might not prevail over them, He would have been comforted by their steadfast faith. But they had not heeded the repeated warning, 'Watch and pray.' . . .

"Just before He bent His footsteps to the garden, Jesus had said to the disciples, 'All ye shall be offended because of Me this night.' They had given Him the strongest assurance that they would go with Him to prison and to death. And poor, self-sufficient Peter had added, 'Although all shall be offended, yet will not I.' Mark 14:27, 29. But the disciples trusted to themselves. They did not look to the mighty Helper as Christ had counseled them to do. Thus when the Saviour was most in need of their sympathy and prayers, they were found asleep. Even Peter was sleeping.

"And John, the loving disciple who had leaned upon the breast of Jesus, was asleep. Surely, the love of John for his Master should have kept him awake. His earnest prayers should have mingled with those of his loved Saviour in the time of His supreme sorrow. The Redeemer had spent entire nights praying for His disciples, that their faith might not fail. . . .

"The disciples awakened at the voice of Jesus, but they hardly knew Him, His face was so changed by anguish. Addressing Peter, Jesus said, 'Simon, sleepest thou? couldest not thou watch one hour? Watch ye and pray, lest ye enter into temptation. The spirit truly is ready, but the flesh is weak.' . . .

"Again the Son of God was seized with superhuman agony, and fainting and exhausted, He staggered back to the place of His former struggle. His suffering was even greater than before. As the agony of soul came upon Him, 'His sweat was as it were great drops of blood falling down to the ground.' The cypress and palm trees were the silent witnesses of His anguish. From their leafy branches dropped heavy dew upon His stricken form, as if nature wept over its Author wrestling alone with the powers of darkness.

"A short time before, Jesus had stood like a mighty cedar, withstanding the storm of opposition that spent its fury upon Him. Stubborn wills, and hearts filled with malice and subtlety, had striven in vain to confuse and overpower Him. He stood forth in divine majesty as the Son of God. Now He was like a reed beaten and bent by the angry storm. He had approached the consummation of His work a conqueror, having at each step gained the victory over the powers of darkness. As one already glorified, He had claimed oneness with God. . . . Now His voice was heard on the still evening air, not in tones of triumph, but full of human anguish. The words of the Saviour were borne to the ears of the drowsy disciples, 'O My Father, if this cup may not pass away from Me, except I drink it, Thy will be done.'

"The first impulse of the disciples was to go to Him; but He had bidden them tarry there, watching unto prayer. When Jesus came to them, He found them still sleeping. Again He had felt a longing for companionship, for some words from His disciples which would bring relief, and break the spell of darkness that well-nigh overpowered Him. But their eyes were heavy; 'neither wist they what to answer Him' " (*The Desire of Ages,* 686–690; see also *Messiah,* 366, 367).

Questions to consider

1. What was at stake for Satan in this struggle in the Garden?

2. Jesus longed for sympathy and encouragement, but the disciples slept. Why did they sleep?

3. If you could have been there to encourage Jesus, what would you have said?

Reflect on the story

"Jesus turned away and fell once more to the ground. The awful moment had come. The eternal fate of the world hung in the balance. Even then, Jesus could have refused to drink the cup that belonged to guilty humans. He could have wiped the bloody sweat from His face and left humans to die in their own sin. He might have said, 'Let the lawbreakers pay the price for sin and I will go back to My Father.' Instead He said for the third time, 'My Father . . . I pray that what You want will be done.'

"Three times Jesus pulled back from making the final decision. But He could see that the human race, if left to itself, was helpless, that sin was too powerful. He saw the misery of a doomed world and the fate its people would suffer. His decision was made. He would save humanity at any cost to Himself. He left heaven to save the one world that had fallen to sin and He would not turn away from His mission now.

"With the decision made, Jesus collapsed, dying, to the ground. But God suffered with His Son. Heaven was silent as the angels watched the Father separate His beams of light, love, and glory from His beloved Son. Satan and his demons watched as well. What would be the answer to Jesus' prayer?

"The answer came when the mightiest angel of heaven rushed to Jesus' side. The angel didn't come to take the cup of suffering away from Jesus, but to strengthen Him with the assurance of His Father's love. He assured Jesus that His death would destroy Satan's kingdom and give this world back to those who followed God. He told Jesus that He would see many of the human race saved eternally.

"Jesus' pain did not go away, but the depression and discouragement did. His bloodstained face now reflected the peace of heaven. He had done what no human could ever do—He had tasted the suffering of death for every person.

"The sleeping disciples suddenly woke up. They saw the angel and heard the words of encouragement and hope he spoke to Jesus. Now they no longer worried for their Master—God was taking care of Him. But again the strange daze came over them, and when Jesus was strong enough to walk to where they were, He found them sleeping again.

"Looking at them sadly, Jesus said, 'Are you still sleeping? The time has come for the Son of man to be handed over to sinful people.' Even as He spoke, He heard the footsteps of the mob that was searching for Him. He called out to the three disciples, ' "Get up, we must go. Look, here comes the man who has turned against me" ' (Matthew 26:46, NCV).

"With no sign of His recent struggle on His face, Jesus stepped out to the crowd and asked, 'Who are you looking for?'

"They answered, 'Jesus of Nazareth.'

" 'I am He,' Jesus replied. As He spoke, the angel who had come to Him stepped between Jesus and the mob. A divine light shone on Jesus' face. This flash of glory staggered the mob and they fell back. Even Judas fell to the ground. Then the angel backed away and the light faded. Jesus could have escaped, but He stood still as the soldiers and priests lay helpless at His feet.

"Their fear, however, didn't last long. Quickly they jumped up and surrounded Jesus, afraid that He would escape. In spite of further glorious evidence that Jesus was the Son of God, they would not believe. Jesus asked again, 'Who are you looking for?'

"They said again, 'Jesus of Nazareth.'

" ' "I told you that I am he," Jesus said. "So if you are looking for me, let the others go" ' (John 18:8,

NCV). He was ready to sacrifice Himself to save His disciples.

"Judas had arranged a signal with the priests to avoid any tricks—he would kiss the person they should arrest. So now he played his part. With the words, 'Greetings, Teacher,' he took Jesus by the hand like a friend, and kissed Him, pretending to weep as if he sympathized with Jesus' situation.

"Jesus said, 'Friend, do what you came to do.' With sadness He asked, 'Judas, are you betraying the Son of man with a kiss?' This should have touched Judas's conscience, but he had no honor or kindness left. Judas had surrendered his will to Satan and could no longer resist him. . . .

"The disciples were terrified that Jesus was allowing Himself to be arrested. They were offended that He and they would be humiliated like that. They couldn't understand and they blamed Jesus for allowing it. In the shock and fear, Peter suggested that they save themselves. So they all left Jesus and ran" (*Messiah*, 367–370; see also *The Desire of Ages*, 693–697).

Questions to consider

1. How many times did Jesus turn away from a final decision? What convinced Him to go on?

2. Why did Judas kiss Jesus?

3. In the Garden, Jesus tasted the total horror of sin. What can help us realize how bad sin is and how much we want to leave it behind forever?

This study is based on Matthew 26:57–75; 27:1, 2, 11–31;
Mark 14:53–72; 15:1–20; Luke 22:54–71; 23:1–25;
John 18:13–40; 19:1–16; and *The Desire of Ages,* chapters 75, 77
—see also *Messiah,* chapters 75, 77.

The rush to convict Jesus

The Jewish leaders had finally arrested Jesus. Now they had to find some criminal charges that would condemn Him to death. And it wouldn't be easy. First, Jesus wasn't guilty of anything other than defying their authority and teaching the people to do the same. Second, under Roman law, the Jewish court could not sentence a person to death. They could only make judgments about cases, which the Roman authorities then had to approve. So the Jewish leaders had to press criminal charges against Jesus that both the Romans and the Jews would accept.

Jesus' first stop on this night of trials was at the palace of Annas, a former high priest. He was the oldest member of the powerful family that controlled the Jewish priests and temple. Before Jesus was tried before the Jewish court—the Sanhedrin—Annas wanted to question Him. Because Joseph of Arimathaea and Nicodemus were suspected of sympathizing with Jesus, they weren't called to the meeting. But the evidence had to be convincing in case others insisted on a fair trial.

Annas had a simple plan. They would charge Jesus with two crimes. If they proved that He blasphemed against God, the Jews would condemn Him. If they proved that He was leading a rebellion, the Romans would condemn Him. Annas tried to trick Jesus into saying that He was planning to secretly set up a new kingdom.

But Jesus saw through Annas's scheme. "I have never taught anything in secret," He said. "I have always taught in the synagogues and in the temple, where all the Jews come together." Then Jesus turned the question on Annas. "Why are you asking Me? Ask your spies who heard Me teach. They know what I said."

Annas was silenced by Jesus' response. But one of his guards hit Jesus in the face. "Is that any way to answer the high priest?" he shouted.

Jesus answered calmly, "If what I said is true, why do you hit Me?"

These trials were even harder for Jesus to bear than they would have been for anyone else. He knew that with His divine power, He could destroy His tormentors in a flash. The Jews were expecting a Messiah who would change people's thoughts and force them to recognize who he was. Jesus was strongly tempted to do just that—to force these priests into admitting that He was their Messiah. It was difficult for Him to set aside His divine power and take their abuse as a human.

The angels of heaven wanted so much to rescue Jesus. As they witnessed the shameful actions of the priests, they were ready to sweep down and destroy them. But they were commanded not to. It was part of Jesus' mission to suffer as a human all the abuse that humans could throw at Him.

One thing was certain. The Jewish leaders had to try Jesus quickly. They had to force an execution quickly, or there would be a week's delay because of the Passover. During such a delay, many would come forward to testify of the miracles Jesus had done. The people might rescue Jesus by force.

Now Jesus was taken before Caiaphas, the current high priest. Caiaphas had come to see Jesus as his rival, and he was jealous of Jesus' popularity with the people. As the Sanhedrin gathered, Jesus was questioned again. But He said nothing. For a time, they faced a dilemma. They had no accusations that would impress the Romans. They called false witnesses, but their testimony was contradictory. Finally, their last chance was to force Jesus to condemn Himself. Caiaphas asked in a solemn oath, "I command you by the power of the living God: Tell us if you are the Messiah, the Son of God."

Jesus knew that answering this question would mean His death. But He had taught His disciples to stand up and tell others who He was. Every eye was locked on His face as He answered. "Those are your words," Jesus said. A heavenly light seemed to illuminate His pale face as He continued, "But in the future, you will see the Son of man sitting at the right hand of God and coming on clouds in the sky."

"This man has said things that are against God!" Caiaphas shouted, ripping his robes. "We don't need any more witnesses. How shall we judge him?"

"He must die!" the other priests and leaders shouted.

Reflect on the story

"The Sanhedrin had pronounced Jesus worthy of death; but it was contrary to the Jewish law to try a prisoner by night. In legal condemnation nothing could be done except in the light of day and before a full session of the council. Notwithstanding this, the Saviour was now treated as a condemned criminal, and given up to be abused by the lowest and vilest of humankind. . . .

"But a keener anguish rent the heart of Jesus; the blow that inflicted the deepest pain no enemy's hand could have dealt. While He was undergoing the mockery of an examination before Caiaphas, Christ had been denied by one of His own disciples.

"After deserting their Master in the garden, two of the disciples had ventured to follow, at a distance, the mob that had Jesus in charge. These disciples were Peter and John. The priests recognized John as a well-known disciple of Jesus, and admitted him to the hall, hoping that as he witnessed the humiliation of his Leader, he would scorn the idea of such a one being the Son of God. John spoke in favor of Peter, and gained an entrance for him also.

"In the court a fire had been kindled; for it was the coldest hour of the night, being just before the dawn. A company drew about the fire, and Peter presumptuously took his place with them. He did not wish to be recognized as a disciple of Jesus. By mingling carelessly with the crowd, he hoped to be taken for one of those who had brought Jesus to the hall.

"But as the light flashed upon Peter's face, the woman who kept the door cast a searching glance upon him. . . . She said to Peter, 'Art not thou also one of this Man's disciples?' Peter was startled and confused; the eyes of the company instantly fastened upon him. He pretended not to understand her; but she was persistent, and said to those around her that this man was with Jesus. Peter felt compelled to answer, and said angrily, 'Woman, I know Him not.' This was the first denial, and immediately the cock crew. . . .

"The disciple John, upon entering the judgment hall, did not try to conceal the fact that he was a follower of Jesus. He did not mingle with the rough company who were reviling his Master. He was not questioned, for he did not assume a false character, and thus lay himself liable to suspicion. He sought a retired corner secure from the notice of the mob, but as near Jesus as it was possible for him to be. Here he could see and hear all that took place at the trial of his Lord.

"Peter had not designed that his real character should be known. In assuming an air of indifference he had placed himself on the enemy's ground, and he became an easy prey to temptation. If he had been called to fight for his Master, he would have been a courageous soldier; but when the finger of scorn was pointed at him, he proved himself a coward. Many who do not shrink from active warfare for their Lord are driven by ridicule to deny their faith. . . .

"Peter tried to show no interest in the trial of his Master, but his heart was wrung with sorrow as he heard the cruel taunts, and saw the abuse He was suffering. . . .

"Attention was called to him the second time, and he was again charged with being a follower of Jesus. He now declared with an oath, 'I do not know the Man.' Still another opportunity was given him. . . . 'Did not I see thee in the garden with Him?' . . . At this Peter flew into a rage. The disciples of Jesus were noted for the purity of their language, and in order fully to deceive his questioners, and justify his assumed character, Peter now denied his Master with cursing and swearing. Again the cock crew. Peter heard it then, and he remembered the words of Jesus, 'Before the cock crow twice, thou shalt deny Me thrice.' Mark 14:30.

"While the degrading oaths were fresh upon Peter's lips, and the shrill crowing of the cock was still ringing in his ears, the Saviour turned from the frowning judges, and looked full upon His poor disciple. At the same time Peter's eyes were drawn to his Master. In that gentle countenance he read deep pity and sorrow, but there was no anger there.

"The sight of that pale, suffering face, those quivering lips, that look of compassion and forgiveness, pierced his heart like an arrow. Conscience was aroused. Memory was active. Peter called to mind his promise of a few short hours before that he would go with his Lord to prison and to death. He remembered his grief when the Saviour told him in the upper chamber that he would deny his Lord thrice that same night. Peter had just declared that he knew not Jesus, but he now realized with bitter grief how well his Lord knew him, and how accurately He had read his heart, the falseness of which was unknown even to himself.

"A tide of memories rushed over him. The Saviour's tender mercy, His kindness and long-suffering, His gentleness and patience toward His erring disciples—all was remembered. . . . He reflected with horror upon his own ingratitude, his falsehood, his perjury. Once more he looked at his Master, and saw a sacrilegious hand raised to smite Him in the face. Unable longer to endure the scene, he rushed, heartbroken, from the hall" (*The Desire of Ages*, 710–713; see also *Messiah*, 376–378).

Questions to consider

1. If you had the power to do so, how hard would it be to refrain from forcing people to choose to do the right thing? If you could force people to obey God and force them to be kind to each other, would you? Why not?

2. Why was Peter accused of being a follower of Jesus but John was ignored?

_____

_____

3. Peter would have been willing to fight for Jesus, but he couldn't bear being criticized for Jesus. Have you ever faced the same struggle?

_____

_____

Reflect on the story

"As soon as it was daylight, the Sanhedrin met again and Jesus was brought back before them. They couldn't condemn Him immediately, because many of those now present had not heard His words at the night meeting. And they knew the Roman authorities would not consider Jesus' words serious enough for a death sentence. But if they could get Jesus to claim to be the Messiah, they might be able to twist His words to sound like a plan to lead a rebellion.

" 'If you are the Messiah, tell us,' they demanded. But Jesus said nothing. They kept badgering Him until He finally said, 'If I tell you, you will not believe Me. And if I ask you, you will not answer.' Then He added a solemn warning. ' "But from now on, the Son of Man will sit at the right hand of the powerful God" ' (Luke 22:69, NCV).

"This was the opening they had hoped for. 'Then are you the Son of God?' they asked.

"Jesus answered, 'You say that I am.'

"This was all they needed. They cried out, 'Why do we need any other witnesses? We heard him say it himself.' So once again, Jesus was condemned to die. All they needed now was for the Roman authorities to agree.

"Once again, this time in the presence of the Jewish priests and leaders, Jesus was beaten and abused. When the judges announced the death sentence, a satanic fury took possession of the people watching, and they rushed toward Jesus. If armed Roman soldiers hadn't stepped in, Jesus would not have lived to be nailed to the cross—He would have been torn to pieces.

"These Roman officers—even though they knew nothing about God—were angry at the brutal treatment of someone who had not been proven guilty of anything. They pointed out that it was against Jewish law to condemn a man to death based on his own testimony. But the Jewish leaders had no shame or pity.

"Priests and leaders forgot the dignity of their offices as they shouted curses at the Son of God. They said that claiming to be the Messiah meant that He should die in the most horrible way. An old coat was thrown over His head and people struck Him in the face, shouting, 'Prove that you are a prophet, you Messiah. Tell us who hit you!'

"Angels recorded every blow, every word, every look of these evil men against their beloved Commander. One day the same men who shouted and spit at the face of Jesus will see it shining with glory brighter than the sun" (_Messiah_, 378, 379; see also _The Desire of Ages_, 714, 715).

Questions to consider

1. What did the Sanhedrin need to get Jesus to say before the Romans would agree to the death sentence?

2. Humans in mobs are often much more violent than they would ever be individually. Why do you think that is? Have you seen an example of mob anger?

Reflect on the story

"When the Saviour was brought into the judgment hall, Pilate looked upon Him with no friendly eyes. The Roman governor had been called from his bedchamber in haste, and he determined to do his work as quickly as possible. He was prepared to deal with the prisoner with magisterial severity. Assuming his severest expression, he turned to see what kind of man he had to examine, that he had been called from his repose at so early an hour. He knew that it must be someone whom the Jewish authorities were anxious to have tried and punished with haste.

"Pilate looked at the men who had Jesus in charge, and then his gaze rested searchingly on Jesus. He had had to deal with all kinds of criminals; but never before had a man bearing marks of such goodness and nobility been brought before him. On His face he saw no sign of guilt, no expression of fear, no boldness or defiance. He saw a man of calm and dignified bearing, whose countenance bore not the marks of a criminal, but the signature of heaven. . . .

"Who is this Man, and wherefore have ye brought Him? he said. What accusation bring ye against Him? The Jews were disconcerted. Knowing that they could not substantiate their charges against Christ, they did not desire a public examination. They answered that He was a deceiver called Jesus of Nazareth. . . .

"The priests thought that with the weak and vacillating Pilate they could carry through their plans without trouble. Before this he had signed the death warrant hastily, condemning to death men they knew were not worthy of death. In his estimation the life of a prisoner was of little account; whether he were innocent or guilty was of no special consequence. The priests hoped that Pilate would now inflict the death penalty on Jesus without giving Him a hearing. This they besought as a favor on the occasion of their great national festival.

"But there was something in the prisoner that held Pilate back from this. He dared not do it. He read the purposes of the priests. He remembered how, not long before, Jesus had raised Lazarus, a man that had been dead four days; and he determined to know, before signing the sentence of condemnation, what were the charges against Him, and whether they could be proved.

"If your judgment is sufficient, he said, why bring the prisoner to me? 'Take ye Him, and judge Him according to your law.' Thus pressed, the priests said that they had already passed sentence upon Him, but that they must have Pilate's sentence to render their condemnation valid. What is your sentence? Pilate asked. The death sentence, they answered; but it is not lawful for us to put any man to death.

A Thoughtful Hour

They asked Pilate to take their word as to Christ's guilt, and enforce their sentence. They would take the responsibility of the result.

"Pilate was not a just or a conscientious judge; but weak though he was in moral power, he refused to grant this request. He would not condemn Jesus until a charge had been brought against Him.

"The priests were in a dilemma. They saw that they must cloak their hypocrisy under the thickest concealment. They must not allow it to appear that Christ had been arrested on religious grounds. Were this put forward as a reason, their proceedings would have no weight with Pilate. They must make it appear that Jesus was working against the common law; then He could be punished as a political offender. Tumults and insurrection against the Roman government were constantly arising among the Jews. . . .

"Now the priests thought to make it appear that on this occasion Christ had taught what they hoped He would teach. In their extremity they called false witnesses to their aid, 'and they began to accuse Him, saying, We found this fellow perverting the nation, and forbidding to give tribute to Caesar, saying that He Himself is Christ a King.' Three charges, each without foundation. The priests knew this, but they were willing to commit perjury could they but secure their end.

"Pilate saw through their purpose. He did not believe that the prisoner had plotted against the government. His meek and humble appearance was altogether out of harmony with the charge. Pilate was convinced that a deep plot had been laid to destroy an innocent man who stood in the way of the Jewish dignitaries. Turning to Jesus he asked, 'Art Thou the King of the Jews?' The Saviour answered, 'Thou sayest it.' And as He spoke, His countenance lighted up as if a sunbeam were shining upon it.

"When they heard His answer, Caiaphas and those that were with him called Pilate to witness that Jesus had admitted the crime with which He was charged. With noisy cries, priests, scribes, and rulers demanded that He be sentenced to death. The cries were taken up by the mob, and the uproar was deafening. Pilate was confused. Seeing that Jesus made no answer to His accusers, Pilate said to Him, 'Answerest Thou nothing? behold how many things they witness against Thee. But Jesus yet answered nothing.'. . .

". . . Hoping to gain the truth from Him and to escape the tumult of the crowd, Pilate took Jesus aside with him, and again questioned, 'Art Thou the King of the Jews?'. . .

" 'My kingdom is not of this world,' He said; 'if My kingdom were of this world, then would My servants fight, that I should not be delivered to the Jews: but now is My kingdom not from hence. Pilate therefore said unto Him, Art Thou a king then? Jesus answered, Thou sayest that I am a king. To this end was I born, and for this cause came I into the world, that I should bear witness unto the truth. Everyone that is of the truth heareth My voice.' . . .

". . . 'What is truth?' he inquired. But he did not wait for an answer. The tumult outside recalled him to the interests of the hour; for the priests were clamorous for immediate action. Going out to the Jews, he declared emphatically, 'I find in Him no fault at all.'

"These words from a heathen judge were a scathing rebuke to the perfidy and falsehood of the rulers of Israel who were accusing the Saviour. As the priests and elders heard this from Pilate, their disappointment and rage knew no bounds. They had long plotted and waited for this opportunity. As they saw the prospect of the release of Jesus, they seemed ready to tear Him in pieces. They loudly denounced Pilate, and threatened him with the censure of the Roman government. They accused him of refusing to condemn Jesus, who, they affirmed, had set Himself up against Caesar.

"Angry voices were now heard, declaring that the seditious influence of Jesus was well known throughout the country. The priests said, 'He stirreth up the people, teaching throughout all Jewry, beginning from Galilee to this place.'

". . . When he heard that Christ was from Galilee, he decided to send Him to Herod, the ruler of that province, who was then in Jerusalem. By this course, Pilate thought to shift the responsibility of the trial from himself to Herod" (*The Desire of Ages,* 723–728; see also *Messiah,* 385–388).

Questions to consider

1. What did Pilate notice first that set Jesus apart from the ordinary criminals he judged?

2. "What is truth?" Pilate asked. Is the truth the same for everyone? Is something that is true for one person always true for another?

3. What threat did the Jewish leaders use against Pilate to force him to find Jesus guilty?

Reflect on the story

"Followed by the jeering mob, Jesus was rushed through the streets of Jerusalem to the palace where Herod was staying. Herod, the same king who had put John the Baptist to death, was delighted to see Jesus. He had heard so much about Him and wanted to see one of His miracles. When Herod first heard about Jesus, he had been afraid that it was John the Baptist come back to life. But now he had the chance to save the life of a prophet and silence the memory of John's death. Herod was sure that Jesus would do whatever he asked in order to be released.

"When the Savior was brought in, the priests quickly began explaining their charges against Him. But Herod commanded them to be silent. He ordered Jesus to be untied and accused the Jews of mistreating the prisoner. He was as quickly convinced as Pilate that Jesus was being falsely accused. Herod began to ask Jesus questions, but Jesus kept silent. At the king's command, sick and lame people were brought in and Jesus was commanded to prove who He was by healing them. Jesus did not respond. Herod kept urging, 'Show us that you have the power we've heard about.'. . .

"Herod promised that if Jesus would perform a miracle, He would be released. The Jewish leaders were terrified that Jesus would do it—certainly they knew that He could. If He did, their plans would be ruined and likely they themselves would be killed. They began to shout, 'He is a traitor and a blasphemer! He works his miracles by the power of the devil!'

"Herod's conscience had been dulled since the days when he trembled at Herodias's request for John the Baptist's head. His loose lifestyle had degraded his morals so badly that he even boasted about killing John. Now he threatened to have Jesus killed if He didn't respond. But Jesus gave no indication that He even heard the words. . . .

"So angry that his face was red, Herod declared that Jesus was an impostor. 'If you won't prove who you claim to be, I will hand you over to the soldiers and the mob. If you are an impostor, you deserve to die. If you are the Son of God, save yourself by working a miracle.'

"At that instant, the crowd leaped at Jesus like wild animals attacking their prey. Jesus was dragged back and forth as Herod joined in trying to humiliate the Son of God. Once again, if the Roman soldiers hadn't stepped in, Jesus would have been torn to pieces. Then Herod had his soldiers wrap a kingly robe around Jesus' shoulders and they joined the Jewish leaders in the worst abuse they could manage. But Jesus still said nothing.

"A few people who came up to mock Jesus turned back, silent and afraid. Even Herod had to step back, suddenly concerned. The last rays of mercy were shining into his sin-hardened heart. Divinity flashed through the human form of Jesus and Herod felt like he was seeing God on His throne. As calloused as he was, he suddenly didn't dare send Jesus to His death. Instead Herod sent Him back to the Roman judgment hall.

"Pilate was disappointed to find the Jews bringing Jesus back. He reminded them that he had already found Jesus innocent. And Herod, a king of their own country, had not agreed to sentence Him. 'I will punish him and let him go free,' he announced. . . .

". . . Then he remembered a custom the Jews cherished that he might use to free Jesus. At Passover time, the Jewish people were often allowed to choose one prisoner to be released from jail. The Romans were holding a prisoner named Barabbas who was already sentenced to die. Barabbas pretended to be a religious revolutionary who was trying to overthrow the Romans. But in reality, he was just a common criminal trying to get rich by robbing others.

"By giving the people a choice between this thief and the clearly innocent Jesus, Pilate was appealing to their sense of justice. He shouted out his question. 'Who do you want me to set free? Barabbas or Jesus, who is called the Messiah?'

"The answer was like the bellow of wild beasts: 'Give us Barabbas!'

"Thinking that they couldn't have understood his question, Pilate asked again, 'Do you want me to free the King of the Jews?'

"The crowd roared even louder. 'Take this man away and set Barabbas free!'

"Pilate cried out, 'Then what should I do with Jesus the Messiah?'

"Demons in human form stood in the crowd and led out in the answering shout: 'Crucify him!'

"Pilate never thought it would come to that. He cringed at the thought of sending an innocent man to that most cruel death. 'Why? What has he done wrong?' he asked. But it was too late for a logical argument. Pilate tried once more to save Jesus. He asked again, 'What has he done wrong?'

"But this only stirred the mob up more. They cried out louder and louder. 'Crucify him! Crucify him!' " (*Messiah*, 388–391; see also *The Desire of Ages*, 728–740).

Questions to consider

1. Both Pilate and Herod had Jesus beaten and let Him die. Why would Jesus speak with Pilate and not with Herod?

2. Why did the Jews choose Barabbas over Jesus?

The Death of Jesus   9

This study is based on Matthew 27:31–53; Mark 15:20–38;
Luke 23:26–46; John 19:16–30; and *The Desire of Ages*, chapter 78
—see also *Messiah*, chapter 78.

On the cross

What would it have been like to stand along the street leading to Calvary? "What's going on?" someone might have called over the noise of the crowd.

"It's Jesus of Nazareth," comes the answer. "They've sentenced Him to death."

"Jesus? The healer? The One some claimed was the Messiah?"

"That's right. They say He declared Himself king and was starting a rebellion against Rome."

Then Jesus Himself staggers into view. He looks like He's aged forty years overnight. He is bruised and bloody, obviously having been beaten and whipped. When the Roman soldiers drop a heavy cross onto His shoulders, He collapses to the street.

"Come on, get up!" voices shout from the crowd. "Carry your cross like a man!" Other voices begin to wail in sorrow at the sight. After a few impatient moments, the soldiers grab a man from the crowd and force him to carry the cross.

You see Jesus lift His head. "Don't cry for Me," He says. "Cry for yourselves and your children." A woman beside you faints and falls to the ground.

Pressing around you are people you recognize from the crowd on the day Jesus rode into Jerusalem on a donkey. The same voices that shouted, "Hosanna!" are now shouting, "Crucify Him!"

You follow to the top of the hill, where the two thieves to be crucified alongside Jesus fight as they are forced onto their crosses. Jesus does not struggle. Averting your eyes as the soldier raises the hammer to drive the spike through His hand, you see His mother. As you watch, she faints and the disciples carry her away.

As close as you are to Jesus, you hear no cry or complaint from Him. You do hear His voice lifted in prayer: "Father, forgive them." Again, you must turn away from the agony on His face as the cross is lifted up and shoved into a hole in the rock.

"If you are the Son of God, come down from there!" comes a shout from beside you. You recoil in horror at the hate in the priest's voice. "If he is the Messiah, let's see him save himself!"

In the midst of the hate and abuse, no one speaks up for Jesus. Will you?

Reflect on the story

"To Jesus in His agony on the cross there came one gleam of comfort. It was the prayer of the penitent thief. Both the men who were crucified with Jesus had at first railed upon Him;

and one under his suffering only became more desperate and defiant. But not so with his companion. This man was not a hardened criminal; he had been led astray by evil associations, but he was less guilty than many of those who stood beside the cross reviling the Saviour. He had seen and heard Jesus, and had been convicted by His teaching, but he had been turned away from Him by the priests and rulers. Seeking to stifle conviction, he had plunged deeper and deeper into sin, until he was arrested, tried as a criminal, and condemned to die on the cross. . . . Among the passers-by he hears many defending Jesus. He hears them repeat His words, and tell of His works. The conviction comes back to him that this is the Christ. Turning to his fellow criminal he says, 'Dost not thou fear God, seeing thou art in the same condemnation?' The dying thieves have no longer anything to fear from man. But upon one of them presses the conviction that there is a God to fear, a future to cause him to tremble. And now, all sin-polluted as it is, his life history is about to close. 'And we indeed justly,' he moans; 'for we receive the due reward of our deeds: but this Man hath done nothing amiss.'

"There is no question now. There are no doubts, no reproaches. When condemned for his crime, the thief had become hopeless and despairing; but strange, tender thoughts now spring up. He calls to mind all he has heard of Jesus, how He has healed the sick and pardoned sin. He has heard the words of those who believed in Jesus and followed Him weeping. He has seen and read the title above the Saviour's head. He has heard the passers-by repeat it, some with grieved, quivering lips, others with jesting and mockery. The Holy Spirit illuminates his mind, and little by little the chain of evidence is joined together. In Jesus, bruised, mocked, and hanging upon the cross, he sees the Lamb of God, that taketh away the sin of the world. Hope is mingled with anguish in his voice as the helpless, dying soul casts himself upon a dying Saviour. 'Lord, remember me,' he cries, 'when Thou comest into Thy kingdom.'

"Quickly the answer came. Soft and melodious the tone, full of love, compassion, and power the words: Verily I say unto thee today, Thou shalt be with Me in Paradise.

"For long hours of agony, reviling and mockery have fallen upon the ears of Jesus. As He hangs upon the cross, there floats up to Him still the sound of jeers and curses. With longing heart He has listened for some expression of faith from His disciples. He has heard only the mournful words, 'We trusted that it had been He which should have redeemed Israel.' How grateful then to the Saviour was the utterance of faith and love from the dying thief! While the leading Jews deny Him, and even the disciples doubt His divinity, the poor thief, upon the brink of eternity, calls Jesus Lord. Many were ready to call Him Lord when He wrought miracles, and after He had risen from the grave; but none acknowledged Him as He hung dying upon the cross save the penitent thief who was saved at the eleventh hour.

"The bystanders caught the words as the thief called Jesus Lord. The tone of the repentant man arrested their attention. Those who at the foot of the cross had been quarreling over Christ's garments, and casting lots upon His vesture, stopped to listen. Their angry tones were hushed. With bated breath they looked upon Christ, and waited for the response from those dying lips.

"As He spoke the words of promise, the dark cloud that seemed to enshroud the cross was pierced by a bright and living light. To the penitent thief came the perfect peace of acceptance with God. Christ in His humiliation was glorified. He who in all other eyes appeared to be conquered was a Conqueror. He was acknowledged as the Sin Bearer. . . .

"I say unto thee today, Thou shalt be with Me in Paradise. Christ did not promise that the thief should be with Him in Paradise that day. He Himself did not go that day to Paradise. He slept in the tomb, and on the morning of the resurrection He said, 'I am not yet ascended to My Father.' John 20:17. But on the day of the crucifixion, the day of apparent defeat and darkness, the promise was given. 'Today' while dying upon the cross as a malefactor, Christ assures the poor sinner, Thou shalt be with Me in Paradise. . . .

"With amazement the angels beheld the infinite love of Jesus, who, suffering the most intense agony of mind and body, thought only of others, and encouraged the penitent soul to believe. In His humiliation He as a prophet had addressed the daughters of Jerusalem; as priest and advocate He had pleaded with the Father to forgive His murderers; as a loving Saviour He had forgiven the sins of the penitent thief" (*The Desire of Ages*, 749–752; see also *Messiah*, 400, 401).

Questions to consider

1. The thief on the cross had heard Jesus teach, but how had he responded? What can happen when you listen to others instead of to the Word of God?

2. What made the thief's words so comforting to Jesus?

3. What facts make it clear that Jesus didn't promise the thief that he would go to paradise that very day?

Reflect on the story

"Now the Lord of glory was near death, feeling agony of both body and soul. It wasn't the fear of death or the pain of the cross that caused His suffering. It was a sense of the horrible wickedness of sin. Jesus saw how few humans would be willing to break their addiction to it. Without help from God, all humans would be exterminated.

"The guilt of every human since Adam was placed on Jesus—our Substitute—and it pressed heavily on His heart. All of His life, Jesus had been sharing the good news of the Father's forgiving love. But now with this terrible weight of sin on Him, He could not see the Father's face. This tore at His heart in a way that humans will never fully understand. This agony was so overwhelming that He hardly felt the physical pain.

"Satan pressed Jesus' heart with fierce temptations. All hope seemed to be gone that He would rise from the grave or that the Father would accept Him. Jesus felt the anguish a sinner will feel when no One pleads for mercy for the guilty. It was this sense of sin—the sense that the Father's anger was focused on Him as the one taking the place of sinful humans—that broke His heart.

"The sun refused to look on this awful scene. Its bright rays had been lighting the earth at noon when suddenly it seemed to be blotted out. The whole land was dark until three o'clock in the afternoon. This unnatural darkness was as deep as midnight without moon or stars. It was a miraculous sign given by God to strengthen our faith.

"God and the holy angels were there beside the cross, hidden in the thick darkness. The Father was with His Son. But His presence had to be hidden. In that terrible hour, Jesus could not be comforted by His Father's presence.

"God created the darkness to cover the last human suffering of His Son. All who had seen Jesus suffer that day had been convicted of His divinity. His long hours of torture had been accompanied by the stares and jeers of the mob. Now, mercifully, God hid Him.

"When the darkness came, an unexplainable terror came over the crowd gathered around the cross. The cursing and shouting stopped. Brilliant lightning occasionally flashed through the clouds and revealed the crucified Savior. Priests, leaders, soldiers, and the mob thought their payback was coming. Some whispered that Jesus would now come down from the cross.

"At three o'clock the darkness lifted from the crowd but still covered Jesus. No one could see through the gloom that shrouded His suffering soul. But Jesus' voice was heard crying, ' "My God, my God, why have you rejected me?" ' (Matthew 27:46, NCV).

"Many voices suggested that Jesus was being punished for claiming to be God. Many of His followers who heard His despairing cry gave up all hope. If God had rejected Jesus, in what could His followers trust?

"Then the darkness lifted and Jesus revived enough to feel the physical pain. He said, 'I am thirsty.' One of the Roman soldiers felt pity and offered Jesus a sponge soaked in vinegar. But the priests mocked Jesus again. They misinterpreted Jesus' cry to mean that He was calling for the prophet Elijah. They refused to relieve His thirst. 'No,' they said, 'we want to see if Elijah will come and save him' " (*Messiah*, 402, 403; see also *The Desire of Ages*, 752–755).

Questions to consider

1. What pain broke Jesus' heart on the cross?

2. Why did the sun dim and a cloud of darkness cover the area? What might it have felt like to be standing there when the sky went dark?

3. Many believers gave up hope when Jesus cried out. What could have held their faith together?

Reflect on the story

"The spotless Son of God hung upon the cross, His flesh lacerated with stripes; those hands so often reached out in blessing, nailed to the wooden bars; those feet so tireless on ministries of love, spiked to the tree; that royal head pierced by the crown of thorns; those quivering lips shaped to the cry of woe. And all that He endured—the blood drops that flowed from His head, His hands, His feet, the agony that racked His frame, and the unutterable anguish that filled His soul at the hiding of His Father's face—speaks to each child of humanity, declaring, It is for thee that the Son of God consents to bear this burden of guilt; for thee He spoils the domain of death, and opens the gates of Paradise. He who stilled the angry waves and walked the foam-capped billows, who made devils tremble and disease flee, who opened blind eyes and called forth the dead to life—offers Himself upon the cross as a sacrifice, and this from love to thee. He, the Sin Bearer, endures the wrath of divine justice, and for thy sake becomes sin itself.

"In silence the beholders watched for the end of the fearful scene. The sun shone forth; but the cross was still enveloped in darkness. Priests and rulers looked toward Jerusalem; and lo, the dense cloud had settled over the city and the plains of Judea. The Sun of Righteousness, the Light of the world, was withdrawing His beams from the once favored city of Jerusalem. The fierce lightnings of God's wrath were directed against the fated city.

"Suddenly the gloom lifted from the cross, and in clear, trumpetlike tones, that seemed to resound throughout creation, Jesus cried, 'It is finished.' 'Father, into Thy hands I commend My spirit.' A light encircled the cross, and the face of the Saviour shone with a glory like the sun. He then bowed His head upon His breast, and died.

"Amid the awful darkness, apparently forsaken of God, Christ had drained the last dregs in the cup of human woe. In those dreadful hours He had relied upon the evidence of His Father's acceptance heretofore given Him. He was acquainted with the character of His Father; He understood His justice, His mercy, and His great love. By faith He rested in Him whom it had ever been His joy to obey. And as in submission He committed Himself to God, the sense of the loss of His Father's favor was withdrawn. By faith, Christ was victor.

"Never before had the earth witnessed such a scene. The multitude stood paralyzed, and with bated breath gazed upon the Saviour. Again darkness settled upon the earth, and a hoarse rumbling, like heavy thunder, was heard. There was a violent earthquake. The people were shaken together in heaps. The wildest confusion and consternation ensued. In the surrounding mountains, rocks were rent asunder, and went crashing down into the plains. Sepulchers were broken open, and the dead were cast out of their tombs. Creation seemed to be shivering to atoms. Priests, rulers, soldiers, executioners, and people, mute with terror, lay prostrate upon the ground.

"When the loud cry, 'It is finished,' came from the lips of Christ, the priests were officiating in the temple. It was the hour of the evening sacrifice. The lamb representing Christ had been brought to be slain. Clothed in his significant and beautiful dress, the priest stood with lifted knife, as did Abraham when he was about to slay his son. With intense interest the people were looking on. But the earth trembles and quakes; for the Lord Himself draws near. With a rending noise the inner veil of the temple is torn from top to bottom by an unseen hand, throwing open to the gaze of the multitude a place once filled with the presence of God. In this place the Shekinah had dwelt. Here God had manifested His glory above the mercy seat. No one but the high priest ever lifted the veil separating this apartment from the rest of the temple. He entered in once a year to make an atonement for the sins of the people. But lo, this veil is rent in twain. The most holy place of the earthly sanctuary is no longer sacred.

"All is terror and confusion. The priest is about to slay the victim; but the knife drops from his nerveless hand, and the lamb escapes. Type has met antitype in the death of God's Son. The great sacrifice has been made. The way into the holiest is laid open. A new and living way is prepared for all. No longer need sinful, sorrowing humanity await the coming of the high priest. Henceforth the Saviour was to officiate as priest and advocate in the heaven of heavens. It was as if a living voice had spoken to the worshipers: There is now an end to all sacrifices and offerings for sin. The Son of God is come according to His word, 'Lo, I come (in the volume of the Book it is written of Me,) to do Thy will, O God.' 'By His own blood' He entereth 'in once into the holy place, having obtained eternal redemption for us.' Hebrews 10:7; 9:12" (*The Desire of Ages*, 755–757, see also *Messiah*, 403, 404).

Questions to consider

1. All that Jesus endured on the cross speaks to each of us. What does it say to you?

2. How did nature respond to the death of its Creator?

3. What happened in the temple as Jesus died?

Jesus Rests 10

This study is based on *The Desire of Ages,* chapter 80
—see also *Messiah,* chapter 80.

The saddest Sabbath

As the long day of shame and torture ended, the saddest and strangest Sabbath since Creation began. Just as He had at the end of Creation, the Son of God rested, His work complete. As it was before sin existed and as it will be when sin is gone forever, the Sabbath of Creation—the day that Jesus rested in the tomb—is a day of rest and rejoicing. From one Sabbath to the next, the saved peoples of the earth will bow in joyful worship of God and of their Savior.

While humans who loved Jesus were weeping, heaven was rejoicing! The plans that had been in place since before the earth existed had been followed. Sin had been defeated, and the human race was saved. It was, as Jesus had said on the cross, finished.

Even as it happened, Jesus' death on the cross led people to see who He really was. A Roman centurion was there to see Jesus' patience as He suffered and His cry of victory when He died. "This Man really was the Son of God," he said. Simon, the man who was forced to carry His cross, became a believer when He saw Jesus respond to hate with love and forgiveness. And the thief who died next to Him declared His faith in Jesus.

Many people that day had flocked to the crucifixion out of curiosity. These Roman executions were entertainment for the masses, and many regularly joined a jeering crowd. Most there that day had been influenced by satanic powers to join in the shouting and mocking. But they didn't hate Jesus.

As the frightening, unnatural darkness lifted, they headed home, feeling guilty of a terrible deed. Many were convinced that Jesus really was the Messiah. But the Jewish leaders still hated Jesus. They thought they had defeated Him, but the darkness and the earthquake shook their confidence. They were more afraid of Jesus dead than alive.

They didn't want His body on the cross during Sabbath, drawing the attention of all those who had gathered in the city for Passover. So they appealed to Pilate. "It would violate our Sabbath for the bodies to stay on the cross. Hurry their deaths so that they can be removed from their crosses before sunset."

Pilate agreed and ordered the soldiers to break the legs of the two thieves so they would die faster. But to the amazement of the priests and leaders, Jesus was already dead. No one before had died on a cross that quickly. To be certain, they asked a soldier to spear Jesus' body in the side.

After the Resurrection, the priests started rumors that Jesus hadn't died on the cross, that He only fainted and was later revived. But the spear wound they had insisted on proved that

Jesus had died. If He hadn't been dead already, the spear would have killed Him.

But it wasn't the spear or the pain of the cross that killed Jesus. He died of a broken heart, a heart broken by the sins of the world.

Reflect on the story

"With the death of Christ the hopes of His disciples perished. They looked upon His closed eyelids and drooping head, His hair matted with blood, His pierced hands and feet, and their anguish was indescribable. Until the last they had not believed that He would die; they could hardly believe that He was really dead. Overwhelmed with sorrow, they did not recall His words foretelling this very scene. Nothing that He had said now gave them comfort. They saw only the cross and its bleeding Victim. The future seemed dark with despair. Their faith in Jesus had perished; but never had they loved their Lord as now. Never before had they so felt His worth, and their need of His presence.

"Even in death, Christ's body was very precious to His disciples. They longed to give Him an honored burial, but knew not how to accomplish this. Treason against the Roman government was the crime for which Jesus was condemned, and persons put to death for this offense were consigned to a burial ground especially provided for such criminals. The disciple John with the women from Galilee had remained at the cross. They could not leave the body of their Lord to be handled by the unfeeling soldiers, and buried in a dishonored grave. Yet they could not prevent it. They could obtain no favors from the Jewish authorities, and they had no influence with Pilate.

"In this emergency, Joseph of Arimathaea and Nicodemus came to the help of the disciples. Both these men were members of the Sanhedrin, and were acquainted with Pilate. Both were men of wealth and influence. They were determined that the body of Jesus should have an honorable burial.

"Joseph went boldly to Pilate, and begged from him the body of Jesus. For the first time, Pilate learned that Jesus was really dead. Conflicting reports had reached him in regard to the events attending the crucifixion, but the knowledge of Christ's death had been purposely kept from him. Pilate had been warned by the priests and rulers against deception by Christ's disciples in regard to His body. Upon hearing Joseph's request, he therefore sent for the centurion who had charge at the cross, and learned for a certainty of the death of Jesus. He also drew from him an account of the scenes of Calvary, confirming the testimony of Joseph.

"The request of Joseph was granted. While John was troubled about the burial of his Master, Joseph returned with Pilate's order for the body of Christ; and Nicodemus came bringing a costly mixture of myrrh and aloes, of about a hundred pounds' weight, for His embalming. The most honored in all Jerusalem could not have been shown more respect in death. The disciples were astonished to see these wealthy rulers as much interested as they themselves in the burial of their Lord.

"Neither Joseph nor Nicodemus had openly accepted the Saviour while He was living. They knew that such a step would exclude them from the Sanhedrin, and they hoped to protect Him by their influence in its councils. For a time they had seemed to succeed; but the wily priests, seeing their favor to Christ, had thwarted their plans. In their absence Jesus had been condemned and delivered to be crucified. Now that He was dead, they no longer concealed their attachment to Him. While the disciples feared to show themselves openly as His followers, Joseph and Nicodemus came boldly to their aid. The help of these rich and honored men was greatly needed at this time. They could do for their dead Master what it was impossible for the poor disciples to do; and their wealth and influence protected them, in a great measure, from the malice of the priests and rulers.

"Gently and reverently they removed with their own hands the body of Jesus from the cross. Their tears of sympathy fell fast as they looked upon His bruised and lacerated form. Joseph owned a new tomb, hewn in a rock. This he was reserving for himself; but it was near Calvary, and he now prepared it for Jesus. The body, together with the spices brought by Nicodemus, was carefully wrapped in a linen sheet, and the Redeemer was borne to the tomb. There the three disciples straightened the mangled limbs, and folded the bruised hands upon the pulseless breast. The Galilean women came to see that all had been done that could be done for the lifeless form of their beloved Teacher. Then they saw the heavy stone rolled against the entrance of the tomb, and the Saviour was left at rest. The women were last at the cross, and last at the tomb of Christ. While the evening shades were gathering, Mary Magdalene and the other Marys lingered about the resting place of their Lord, shedding tears of sorrow over the fate of Him whom they loved. 'And they returned, . . . and rested the Sabbath day according to the commandment.' Luke 3:56" (*The Desire of Ages*, 772–774; see also *Messiah*, 412, 413).

Questions to consider

1. Why hadn't Nicodemus or Joseph of Arimathaea publicly followed Jesus before He died? Is it OK to hide our true agenda from the public if it helps the church's cause?

2. Imagine being one of the disciples that Sabbath. What would you look forward to? Where would you go next? Could you continue to believe in God if Jesus was dead?

Reflect on the story

"It was an unforgettable Sabbath for the disciples, the priests and leaders, and the people of Jerusalem. The Passover was observed as it had been for centuries while the One it pointed to lay in Joseph's tomb. The courts of the temple were filled with people. The high priest was there in his fine robe; the other priests performed their duties.

"But there was a sense of strangeness to everything. The people were not aware that Jesus' death had fulfilled the prophecies and the symbols of the Passover service. But they had conflicting feelings as they witnessed the service this time. The Most Holy Place—the heart of the temple that only the high priests had ever seen—was now open to be seen by anyone. No longer considered a holy place by God, its curtain had been ripped from top to bottom. This worried the priests greatly—they were sure that something terrible was going to happen.

"During these hours between the Crucifixion and the Resurrection many sleepless people studied the prophecies. Some searched for evidence that Jesus was not who He claimed to be. Others searched for proof that He was the Messiah. Regardless of where they started, they all arrived at the same conclusion: the One

A Thoughtful Hour

who had been crucified was the Savior of the world. Many of them never again celebrated Passover. Even among the priests, many searched the prophecies and after His resurrection, they followed Jesus as the Son of God.

"Nicodemus remembered Jesus' words spoken that night on the Mount of Olives: ' "Just as Moses lifted up the snake in the desert, the Son of Man must also be lifted up. So that everyone who believes can have eternal life in him" ' (John 3:14, 15, NCV). The meaning of these words were no longer a mystery to him. Nicodemus regretted not becoming a follower of Jesus while He was still alive. He had heard Jesus' words for His murderers and to the dying thief and they touched his heart. When Jesus called out, 'It is finished,' in a triumphant voice, Nicodemus's faith was settled. The Cross destroyed the hopes of the disciples, but it convinced Joseph and Nicodemus that Jesus truly was the Son of God.

"Jesus was never more popular with the crowds than He was now that He was dead. People brought their sick loved ones to the temple courts, calling out, 'We want Jesus, the Healer!' But His healing hands were folded on His chest. So many people were asking loudly for Jesus, that the priests finally had them driven out of the temple courts. Then they stationed soldiers at the gates to keep out the crowds. Those who were looking for help were crushed with disappointment. The sick were dying without Jesus' healing touch.

"Thousands were convinced that a great light in the world had gone out. Without Jesus, the earth was dark. Many who had shouted 'Crucify him, crucify him' now realized what a terrible thing they had done.

"When the people learned that Jesus had been executed, they started asking questions. In spite of their attempts to keep it private, reports of how Jesus was treated during His trials spread everywhere. Respected thinkers asked the priests and leaders to explain the prophecies of the Messiah. Of course, the priests couldn't explain the prophecies that pointed to the Messiah's suffering and death. They nearly went mad trying to create a lie for an answer.

"The priests knew they were being severely criticized by the people. The ones they had influenced to shout out against Jesus were now horrified by their shameful behavior. But worse than that, the priests were terrified that Jesus would rise from His grave and appear to them again. They remembered His words: 'Destroy this temple and I will raise it up again in three days.' Judas had told them Jesus' prediction that He would be betrayed and condemned by the priests, that He would be killed and would rise again on the third day. They remembered that Jesus' predictions had always been fulfilled before. Who could say that this wouldn't happen also?

"As much as the priests wanted to shut out these thoughts, they could not. In their minds they could see Jesus, calm and quiet before them, suffering their taunts and abuse without a word. They were struck with the overwhelming thought that He really was the Son of God. At any moment He might appear, accusing them, demanding justice, and demanding the death of His murderers.

"Even though it broke their Sabbath rules, they held a council meeting to discuss what to do about Jesus' body. Then the Pharisees and priests went to Pilate with a request. 'When that liar was still alive, he said, "I will rise again in three days." Command your soldiers to seal and guard his tomb for at least three days so his disciples don't steal his body away and tell everyone that he is alive again.'

"Pilate agreed, and the soldiers did as the priests directed. Ropes were stretched across the stone that covered the tomb, and they were sealed with a Roman seal. Then one hundred soldiers were stationed

64

around the tomb. Now no one could move the stone without the permission of Rome. Jesus was sealed in His tomb as securely as if He would be there for all time.

"But the efforts made to prevent Jesus' resurrection became the most convincing arguments to prove it. The more soldiers stationed around His tomb, the greater the story would be. Roman weapons were powerless to keep the Lord of life in the tomb. The time of His release was near" (*Messiah*, 413–415; see also *The Desire of Ages*, 774–778).

Questions to consider

1. What happened on that uneasy Sabbath as many people studied the prophecies?

2. Why did so many wait until after Jesus' death before questioning the priests about the prophecies concerning the Messiah? Why do we wait for a crisis before we focus on the things of God?

3. What did the soldiers do to secure Jesus' tomb? How did those efforts become the strongest evidence of His resurrection?

Resurrection Morning 11

This study is based on Matthew 28:1–8, 11–15; Mark 16:1–8;
Luke 24:1–12; John 20:1–18; and *The Desire of Ages,* chapters 81, 82
—see also *Messiah,* chapters 81, 82.

The Resurrection

There is no scene in Scripture more powerful than the resurrection of Jesus. In a few short words, the universe is forever changed! As you read those words, place yourself there at dawn. Could you even grasp the things you saw? Would you even believe your eyes?

Reflect on the story

"The night before the first day of the week had worn slowly away. Jesus was still a prisoner in His tomb. The Roman guards were still on watch. Their seal was unbroken. If it were possible, the prince of darkness would have kept that tomb sealed forever. But powerful heavenly angels were waiting to welcome their Prince back to life.

"As dawn lighted up the eastern sky, a great earthquake shook the world. A flash of glory split the sky as heaven's mightiest angel came down and rolled the stone away from the tomb as if it were a pebble. As the rest of the angel armies surrounded the tomb, Satan's hosts fled. The normally brave Roman soldiers trembled, acting like they had been captured without so much as a fight.

"Then the angel cried, 'Son of God, come out! Your Father is calling You!'

"Out of the darkness of the tomb stepped Jesus, the Messiah, the Savior, the glorified Son of God. In a mighty voice that could no longer be silent, He proclaimed, 'I am the Resurrection and the Life!' As He stepped out, clothed in His divine majesty and glory, the angel army greeted Him with songs of praise.

"The Roman soldiers fainted away like dead men.

"When the heavenly beings vanished, the soldiers rose up and staggered as drunk men to the city, telling everyone they met what they had seen. They were headed to Pilate to report, but the priests and leaders intercepted them and insisted on hearing their story first. Still trembling with fear, their faces as white as sheets, they told everything just as they had seen it. They said, 'It was the Son of God who was crucified! We heard the angel announce Him as the King of heaven!'

"Panicked, Caiaphas tried to speak. His lips moved, but no sounds came out. The soldiers were about to leave when finally he found his voice. 'Wait, wait!' he cried. 'Tell no one what you saw.'

"The other priests joined in. 'Tell everyone that His disciples stole the body while you were sleeping.' The priests had outsmarted themselves here. If the soldiers were asleep, how could they know what happened? And if the disciples had stolen the body, wouldn't the priests be demanding their arrest? And wouldn't they also be demanding that the soldiers be arrested for sleeping?

"The soldiers were horrified at the suggestion. Sleeping on duty was punishable by death. Why should they lie and risk their lives?

"The priests promised that the soldiers would not be punished. After all, Pilate would not want their story spread any more than the priests did. So the Roman soldiers sold out. They went to the priests carrying only a shocking but true report; they left carrying money and lies" (*Messiah*, 416, 417; see also *The Desire of Ages*, 779–782).

Questions to consider

1. If you had seen the angel army gather, would you have suspected that they were there to welcome Jesus with singing? Imagine hearing that song!

2. How had the priests outsmarted themselves? Why would the soldiers hesitate to lie and say they had fallen asleep?

Reflect on the story

"When the voice of the mighty angel was heard at Christ's tomb, saying, Thy Father calls Thee, the Saviour came forth from the grave by the life that was in Himself. Now was proved the truth of His words, 'I lay down My life, that I might take it again. . . . I have power to lay it down, and I have power to take it again.' Now was fulfilled the prophecy He had spoken to the priests and rulers, 'Destroy this temple, and in three days I will raise it up.' John 10:17, 18; 2:19.

"Over the rent sepulcher of Joseph, Christ had proclaimed in triumph, 'I am the resurrection, and the life.' These words could be spoken only by the Deity. All created beings live by the will and power of God. They are dependent recipients of the life of God. From the highest seraph to the humblest animate being, all are replenished from the Source of life. Only He who is one with God could say, I have power to lay down My life, and I have power to take it again. In His divinity, Christ possessed the power to break the bonds of death.

"Christ arose from the dead as the first fruits of those that slept. He was the antitype of the wave sheaf, and His resurrection took place on the very day when the wave sheaf was to be presented before the Lord. For more than a thousand years this symbolic ceremony had been performed. From the harvest fields the first heads of ripened grain were gathered, and when the people went up to Jerusalem to the Passover, the sheaf of first fruits was waved as a thank offering before the Lord. Not until this was presented could the sickle be put to the grain, and it be gathered into sheaves. The sheaf dedicated to God represented the harvest. So Christ the first fruits represented the great spiritual harvest to be gathered for the kingdom of God. His resurrection is the type and pledge of the resurrection of all the righteous dead. 'For if we believe that Jesus died and rose again, even so them also which sleep in Jesus will God bring with Him.' 1 Thessalonians 4:14.

"As Christ arose, He brought from the grave a multitude of captives. The earthquake at His death had rent open their graves, and when He arose, they came forth with Him. They were those who had been co-laborers with God, and who at the cost of their lives had borne testimony to the truth. Now they were to be witnesses for Him who had raised them from the dead. . . .

"These went into the city, and appeared unto many, declaring, Christ has risen from the dead, and we be risen with Him. . . .

"To the believer, Christ is the resurrection and the life. In our Saviour the life that was lost through sin is restored; for He has life in Himself to quicken whom He will. He is invested with the right to give immortality. The life that He laid down in humanity, He takes up again, and gives to humanity. 'I am come,' He said, 'that they might have life, and that they might have it more abundantly.' . . .

"The voice that cried from the cross, 'It is finished,' was heard among the dead. It pierced the walls of sepulchers, and summoned the sleepers to arise. Thus will it be when the voice of Christ shall be heard from heaven. That voice will penetrate the graves and unbar the tombs, and the dead in Christ shall arise. At the Saviour's resurrection a few graves were opened, but at His second coming all the precious dead shall hear His voice, and shall come forth to glorious, immortal life. The same power that raised Christ from the dead will raise His church, and glorify it with Him, above all principalities, above all powers, above every name that is named, not only in this world, but also in the world to come" (*The Desire of Ages*, 785–787; see also *Messiah*, 418, 419).

Questions to consider

1. Why was it important that Jesus raised Himself from the dead?

2. How did Jesus' resurrection have the same meaning as the "wave sheaf"? What was the "wave sheaf"?

3. What does the promise of the resurrection mean to you? Whom do you long to see on that day?

"Why are you crying?"

After the saddest Sabbath of their lives, the women who had been at the cross headed to Jesus' tomb at first light. There was no thought of His rising from the tomb—they were going to wash His body with oils and perfume, something they had run out of time to do as they buried Him on Friday evening.

The women had come from different directions, but as they entered the garden, their only thought was, *Who will roll the stone away from the tomb for us?* They lurched as the ground shook and shielded their eyes when the sky blazed with glory. *What was that?* they wondered.

Mary Magdalene reached Jesus' tomb first and saw that it was open, that the stone had been rolled back. She turned and rushed away to tell the disciples. As the other women arrived, they saw a glow around the tomb, but Jesus' body was gone.

Suddenly, they noticed that they were not alone. What appeared to be a young man in white, shining clothes was sitting nearby. It was really the angel who had rolled away the stone. "Don't be afraid," he said. "I know you are looking for Jesus, but He's not here. He has risen from the dead just as He said He would."

They looked into the tomb and saw another young man. "Why are you looking for a living person in this tomb?" the angel asked. "He's not here—He's alive! Remember—He said that He would be crucified, but then He would rise from the dead on the third day."

So these faithful women—not even given names in Scripture—were the first to hear the news that Jesus was alive.

Reflect on the story

"Mary had not heard the good news. She went to Peter and John with the sorrowful message, 'They have taken away the Lord out of the sepulcher, and we know not where they have laid Him.' The disciples hurried to the tomb, and found it as Mary had said. They saw the shroud and the napkin, but they did not find their Lord. Yet even here was testimony that He had risen. The graveclothes were not thrown heedlessly aside, but carefully folded, each in a place by itself. John 'saw, and believed.' He did not yet understand the scripture that Christ must rise from the dead; but he now remembered the Saviour's words foretelling His resurrection.

"It was Christ Himself who had placed those graveclothes with such care. When the mighty angel came down to the tomb, he was joined by another, who with his company had been keeping guard over the Lord's body. As the angel from heaven rolled away the stone, the other entered the tomb, and unbound the wrappings from the body of Jesus. But it was the Saviour's hand that folded each, and laid it in its place. In His sight who guides alike the star and the atom, there is nothing unimportant. Order and perfection are seen in all His work.

"Mary had followed John and Peter to the tomb; when they returned to Jerusalem, she remained. As she looked into the empty tomb, grief filled her heart. Looking in, she saw the two angels, one at the head and the other at the foot where Jesus had lain. 'Woman, why weepest thou?' they asked her. 'Because they have taken away my Lord,' she answered, 'and I know not where they have laid Him.'

"Then she turned away, even from the angels, thinking that she must find someone who could tell her what had been done with the body of Jesus. Another voice addressed her, 'Woman, why weepest thou? whom seekest thou?' Through her tear-dimmed eyes, Mary saw the form of a man, and thinking that it was the gardener, she said, 'Sir, if thou have borne Him hence, tell me where thou hast laid Him, and I will take Him away.' If this rich man's tomb was thought too honorable a burial place for Jesus, she herself would provide a place for Him. There was a grave that Christ's own voice had made vacant, the grave where Lazarus had lain. Might she not there find a burial place for her Lord? She felt that to care for His precious crucified body would be a great consolation to her in her grief.

"But now in His own familiar voice Jesus said to her, 'Mary.' Now she knew that it was not a stranger who was addressing her, and turning she saw before her the living Christ. In her joy she forgot that He had been crucified. Springing toward Him, as if to embrace His feet, she said, 'Rabboni.' But Christ raised His hand, saying, Detain Me not; 'for I am not yet ascended to My Father: but go to My brethren, and say unto them, I ascend unto My Father, and your Father; and to My God, and your God.' And Mary went her way to the disciples with the joyful message" (*The Desire of Ages*, 789, 790; see also *Messiah*, 420–422).

Questions to consider

1. How were Jesus' folded grave clothes evidence that He was alive?

2. Mary recognized that it was Jesus by His voice. Is it possible for us to recognize the voice of Jesus? How can we learn to do this?

3. Why would the disciples not believe the reports of Mary and the other women?

4. What was Jesus' first work after His resurrection?

Reflect on the story

"The angels had told the women, ' "Now go and tell his followers and Peter, 'Jesus is going into Galilee ahead of you, and you will see him there as he told you before' " ' (Mark 16:7, NCV). This message from angels should have convinced the disciples. Words like these could only come from messengers of their Master. . . .

"When Mary told the disciples that she had seen Jesus, she repeated this call to a meeting in Galilee. And the message was sent a third time when Jesus appeared to other women saying, 'Tell My brothers to go to Galilee and they will see Me there.'

"Jesus' first work after His resurrection was to convince His disciples that His love for them had not changed. He wanted to draw them even closer. That's why He planned to meet them in Galilee.

"But the disciples still doubted. When the women claimed that they had seen Jesus, the disciples thought they were seeing things. In their minds, troubles were piling onto troubles. They had seen their Master die, His body was missing, and they were being accused of stealing it to deceive the crowds. They felt they could never straighten out the lies that were being spread. They were afraid of the priests and of the crowds. They longed for the presence of Jesus.

"They kept repeating the words, ' "We were hoping that he would free Israel" ' (Luke 24:21, NCV). Lonely and heartbroken, they met together in an upstairs room with the doors closed and locked, knowing that the fate of their beloved Teacher might be theirs at any moment. And all the time they could have been celebrating the news that Jesus was alive.

"Many today do the same thing. Jesus is right beside them, but their tear-filled eyes do not see Him. He speaks to them, but they do not understand.

"We should listen and do what the angel told Jesus' disciples: 'Go quickly and tell His followers that He is alive!' Don't bother looking at the empty grave. Let the song ring out across the world: 'Jesus is risen!' He lives and represents us in heaven before the Father!" (*Messiah*, 422, 423; see also *The Desire of Ages*, 793, 794).

Questions to consider

1. Is it significant that Jesus appeared first to women and gave them a message to the disciples? Why would the disciples not believe the reports of Mary and the other women?

2. Do we ever do make the same mistake the disciples made—remaining lonely and depressed when Jesus is right beside us?

"We Have Seen Him!"

This study is based on Luke 24:13–48; John 20:19–29;
and *The Desire of Ages,* chapters 83, 84
—see also *Messiah,* chapters 83, 84.

The Stranger

Late in the afternoon on the day of the Resurrection, two of Jesus' disciples were walking home to Emmaus, a small town about eight miles from Jerusalem. These were not two of the twelve who had followed Jesus most closely. They were of the many others who had listened and learned from Jesus—ones who saw that He was their Hope, that He was their Savior.

As they walked, a Stranger joined them. They continued their conversation, talking about Jesus. They wondered whether this Man, who had suffered so much shame, could really be the Messiah.

"What are you talking about?" the Stranger asked.

"You must be the only person in Jerusalem who doesn't know what's been happening," the man named Cleopas answered. They told the Stranger all about Jesus. "He was a prophet who did many powerful things. Our leaders handed Him over to the Romans to be killed." With great sadness, they added, "We were hoping that He was the Messiah. And this is the third day since it happened."

Starting at the beginning of Scripture, the Stranger mentioned all the Scriptures that pointed to the Messiah. The Stranger was Jesus, but He didn't tell them who He was. To build their faith, He convinced them from the writings of the prophets that His death was the strongest evidence for their faith in Him as the Messiah.

Instead of the Messiah who would rule like a king, they needed to understand that the Messiah had to die. It would end in victory, but the path to save the world from sin would be a hard one.

When they arrived in Emmaus, Jesus acted as if He would continue traveling on down the road. "Come in and stay with us," they urged Him. If they hadn't, they would never have known who the Stranger really was.

They sat at the table to eat, and the Stranger lifted His hands to bless the food—exactly as Jesus had always done. The disciples stared in astonishment. They looked again and saw the prints of nails in His hands. Both of them shouted, "It is Jesus!"

As they jumped up, He vanished. Looking at the empty chair, they said to each other, "We should have known it was Him!" Forgetting about being tired and hungry, they left their meal on the table and hurried back to Jerusalem to share their amazing news with the other disciples.

Because it was Passover, Jerusalem's eastern gate was still open even though it was already dark. Only a few houses showed the flickering of a lamp in a window as the two disciples hurried through the streets. They knew where to go—local believers knew that Jesus' closest followers were in hiding in the same upstairs room where they had shared the Last Supper with Him.

Racing up the stairs to the door, they knocked loudly as they labored to catch their breath. There was no answer. They knocked again, but got no response. Finally, Cleopas called out their names. Slowly, quietly, the lock on the door slid back. The door squeaked open just wide enough for the two to enter. No one saw the hidden Companion who also came inside. The door was quickly locked again to keep spies out.

As they entered, the two men found the room in an uproar. "The Lord really has risen! He appeared to Peter!" someone said loudly. "It can't be true," hissed another. "The priests stole His body."

Cleopas raised his hands. "We have seen Him!" With faces still flushed from their journey, the two travelers told how Jesus had walked with them to Emmaus. "We didn't know it was Jesus who was traveling with us," they explained. "But He told us how the Scriptures foretold His death."

"That's too good to be true," someone said. "I don't believe it," said another.

And suddenly, He was there. No one had knocked, there had been no footsteps, but there He stood.

Everyone in the room froze, hardly even breathing. Then they heard the voice they knew, the voice of their Teacher and Friend. "Peace be with you," Jesus said.

But not everyone felt peace. "It's a ghost," someone moaned. Others collapsed to the floor in shock.

Jesus shook His head. " 'Why are you troubled? Why do you doubt what you see? Look at my hands and my feet. It is I myself!' " (Luke 24:38, 39, NCV). They still stared at Him, hardly able to believe it. Jesus asked, "Is there any food here?" Someone brought Him a piece of broiled fish, and as they watched, Jesus ate it.

That was enough. Now faith took over the doubt in their hearts. Jesus was alive! He had really risen from the dead!

Reflect on the story

"When Jesus met with His disciples, He reminded them of the words He had spoken to them before His death, that all things must be fulfilled which were written in the law of Moses, and in the prophets, and in the Psalms concerning Him. . . .

"The disciples began to realize the nature and extent of their work. They were to proclaim to the world the wonderful truths which Christ had entrusted to them. The events of His life, His death and resurrection, the prophecies that pointed to these events, the sacredness of the law of God, the mysteries of the plan of salvation, the power of Jesus for the remission of sins—to all these things they were witnesses, and they were to make them known to the world. They were to proclaim the gospel of peace and salvation through repentance and the power of the Saviour.

" 'And when He had said this, He breathed on them, and saith unto them, Receive ye the Holy Ghost.' . . .

"The Holy Spirit is the breath of spiritual life in the soul. The impartation of the Spirit is the impartation of the life of Christ. It imbues the receiver with the attributes of Christ. Only those who are thus taught of God, those who possess the inward working of the Spirit, and in whose life the Christ-life is manifested, are to stand as representative men, to minister in behalf of the church.

" 'Whosoever sins ye remit,' said Christ, 'they are remitted; . . . and whosoever sins ye retain, they are retained.' Christ here gives no liberty for any man to pass judgment upon others. In the Sermon on the Mount He forbade this. It is the prerogative of God. But on the church in its organized capacity

He places a responsibility for the individual members. Toward those who fall into sin, the church has a duty, to warn, to instruct, and if possible to restore. 'Reprove, rebuke, exhort,' the Lord says, 'with all long-suffering and doctrine.' 2 Timothy 4:2. Deal faithfully with wrongdoing. Warn every soul that is in danger. Leave none to deceive themselves. Call sin by its right name. Declare what God has said in regard to lying, Sabbathbreaking, stealing, idolatry, and every other evil. 'They which do such things shall not inherit the kingdom of God.' Galatians 5:21. If they persist in sin, the judgment you have declared from God's word is pronounced upon them in heaven. In choosing to sin, they disown Christ; the church must show that she does not sanction their deeds, or she herself dishonors her Lord. . . .

"But there is a brighter side to the picture. 'Whosoever sins ye remit, they are remitted.' Let this thought be kept uppermost. In labor for the erring, let every eye be directed to Christ. Let the shepherds have a tender care for the flock of the Lord's pasture. Let them speak to the erring of the forgiving mercy of the Saviour. Let them encourage the sinner to repent, and believe in Him who can pardon. Let them declare, on the authority of God's word, 'If we confess our sins, He is faithful and just to forgive us our sins, and to cleanse us from all unrighteousness.' 1 John 1:9. All who repent have the assurance, 'He will have compassion upon us; He will subdue our iniquities; and Thou wilt cast all their sins into the depths of the sea.' Micah 7:19.

"Let the repentance of the sinner be accepted by the church with grateful hearts. Let the repenting one be led out from the darkness of unbelief into the light of faith and righteousness. Let his trembling hand be placed in the loving hand of Jesus. Such a remission is ratified in heaven.

"Only in this sense has the church power to absolve the sinner. Remission of sins can be obtained only through the merits of Christ. To no man, to no body of men, is given power to free the soul from guilt. Christ charged His disciples to preach the remission of sins in His name among all nations; but they themselves were not empowered to remove one stain of sin. The name of Jesus is the only 'name under heaven given among men, whereby we must be saved.' Acts 4:12" (*The Desire of Ages*, 804–806; see also *Messiah*, 429, 430).

Questions to consider

1. Why would Jesus have appeared to two "unknown" disciples before He appeared to the group? What does that mean to us, who are not as "known" as some Christian leaders?

2. What was the reaction of the disciples when Jesus appeared among them in the room? What did Jesus do to convince them that He was real?

3. The disciples had to share with the world what they had seen and heard. Is that our job as well? What have you seen and heard that you can share?

4. What is the difference between a person judging others and the church acting to reprove and correct sinners? Can a church also be guilty of judging others?

Reflect on the story

"When Jesus met the disciples in that upstairs room, Thomas was not with them. He heard the stories from the others about Jesus, but his heart was still filled with gloom and doubt. Even if Jesus had really risen, there was no longer any hope of seeing His kingdom on earth. And he was hurt to think that Jesus would show Himself to everyone else except him. Thomas decided not to believe and for a whole week he sulked sadly.

"Over and over Thomas declared, 'I will not believe it until I see the nail marks in His hands for myself, until I can touch those scars and the scar on His side.' He had no faith in what the others told him. Thomas loved his Lord, but he allowed jealousy and doubt to control his heart.

"One evening Thomas agreed to meet with the others in the usual room for supper. He still had a faint hope that the good news was true. As they ate, the disciples talked about the things Jesus had shown them from the prophecies. Suddenly, even though the door was locked, Jesus appeared in the middle of the group and said, 'Peace be with you.'

"Then He turned to Thomas. 'Look at My hands. Touch them with your finger. Put your hand on the scar on My side. Stop doubting and believe!'

"Thomas knew that none of the others had told Jesus about his words of doubt. Clearly Jesus knew even his thoughts. He didn't need any other proof. His heart leaped with joy as he fell down at Jesus' feet and said, 'My Lord and my God.'

"Jesus accepted Thomas's words, but He gently scolded him for his doubts. ' "You believe because you see me. Those who believe without seeing me will be truly happy" ' (John 20:29, NCV). If we followed Thomas's example, no one would believe, because we all must learn about Jesus from someone else. Many who—like Thomas—insist on having all their doubts removed will never find the answers they seek. Doubting will eventually become what they believe in most. Then when they urgently need faith and confidence in God, they will find themselves unable to hope and believe.

"The way Jesus treated Thomas also shows us how to treat those who express their doubts publicly. In spite of Thomas's unreasonable demands, Jesus showed him what he asked for. Doubt rarely can be argued away. What any doubter needs to see is Jesus, the crucified Savior, in all His love and mercy" (*Messiah*, 430, 431; see also *The Desire of Ages*, 806–808).

Questions to consider

1. What happens if we insist that all our doubts be removed, all our questions answered? What doubts do you still have?

2. How should we treat those who raise questions or doubts about God or religion?

By the Lake Again   13

This study is based on John 21:1–22 and *The Desire of Ages,* chapter 85
—see also *Messiah,* chapter 85.

Fishermen again

The disciples were stuck in Jerusalem. Jesus had promised to meet them in Galilee, but they couldn't leave the city. Passover lasted an entire week, and if they left the Holy City before it ended, people would notice and would accuse them of leaving their Jewish faith as well.

How frustrating that must have been! How anxious they were to leave, to follow Jesus' direction to meet Him!

When the week finally ended, they headed north. They couldn't all travel together, but several went with Peter, James, and John back to their hometown of Capernaum. They found a quiet place where they wouldn't be disturbed and stood looking out over the Sea of Galilee. For three years they had followed Jesus, learning from the greatest Teacher. Now they were not just fishermen, but teachers themselves.

How did it feel standing there next to the water they had fished so many times? Did the water look different after seeing Jesus walk on it? Did the wind feel the same knowing that Jesus could control it with a word? From where they stood they could see the beach where thousands had been fed from only a few small loaves of bread and fishes. Would they ever see such things again?

As amazing as their lives had been for the past three years, at this moment they were unemployed and very poor. But they hadn't forgotten everything from their past. "We still have boats and nets here," Peter said. "Let's go fishing. A good catch will buy us a few meals and maybe a new cloak."

Tossing fishing nets into the lake through the night must have seemed like going home again. But on this night, they caught nothing. Through the long, dark hours they talked about Jesus, about the things that had happened, and what those things meant. As amazing and glorious as it was that Jesus had returned from the dead, it was clear that their lives of following Him from village to village were over.

Again and again, they came to the questions: "What happens now? Where do we go from here?" Their futures seemed as murky as the dark water.

As dawn brightened the sky, the boat was near the shore. A stranger called out to the disciples from the beach. "Friends, did you catch any fish?"

"No," they answered.

"Throw your nets out on this side, toward me," he called back. "Then you will catch some." With a shrug, they did—and suddenly the net was so full that they couldn't pull it back into the boat.

John recognized that voice. "It's Jesus!" he exclaimed to Peter. As Peter had done once before on this lake, he jumped into the water and headed toward Jesus. This time, he could wade to shore. The others brought the boat in, pulling the net that was so full of fish.

Jesus waited near a fire of hot coals. "Bring some of your fish," He said.

Peter rushed out into the water to help drag the net to shore. After the work was done, Jesus served the cooked food to each of them. The disciples had talked about Jesus all night, but in His presence they could find nothing to say. They ate quietly.

All they could think of was the day that Jesus had called them out of their fishing boats and asked them to follow Him. He had performed the same fishing miracle that time. Was He telling them that nothing had changed about the "fishing" He had called them to do? Was He promising that if they continued to do His work, He would provide for their needs?

Reflect on the story

"Another lesson Christ had to give, relating especially to Peter. Peter's denial of his Lord had been in shameful contrast to his former professions of loyalty. He had dishonored Christ, and had incurred the distrust of his brethren. They thought he would not be allowed to take his former position among them, and he himself felt that he had forfeited his trust. Before being called to take up again his apostolic work, he must before them all give evidence of his repentance. Without this, his sin, though repented of, might have destroyed his influence as a minister of Christ. The Saviour gave him opportunity to regain the confidence of his brethren, and, so far as possible, to remove the reproach he had brought upon the gospel.

"Here is given a lesson for all Christ's followers. The gospel makes no compromise with evil. It cannot excuse sin. Secret sins are to be confessed in secret to God; but, for open sin, open confession is required. The reproach of the disciple's sin is cast upon Christ. It causes Satan to triumph, and wavering souls to stumble. By giving proof of repentance, the disciple, so far as lies in his power, is to remove this reproach.

"While Christ and the disciples were eating together by the seaside, the Saviour said to Peter, 'Simon, son of Jonas, lovest thou Me more than these?' referring to his brethren. Peter had once declared, 'Though all men shall be offended because of Thee, yet will I never be offended.' Matthew 26:33. But he now put a truer estimate upon himself. 'Yea, Lord,' he said, 'Thou knowest that I love Thee.' There is no vehement assurance that his love is greater than that of his brethren. He does not express his own opinion of his devotion. To Him who can read all the motives of the heart he appeals to judge as to his sincerity, 'Thou knowest that I love Thee.' And Jesus bids him, 'Feed My lambs.'

"Again Jesus applied the test to Peter, repeating His former words: 'Simon, son of Jonas, lovest thou Me?' This time He did not ask Peter whether he loved Him better than did his brethren. The second response was like the first, free from extravagant assurance: 'Yea, Lord; Thou knowest that I love Thee.' Jesus said to him, 'Feed My sheep.' Once more the Saviour put the trying question: 'Simon, son of Jonas, lovest thou Me?' Peter was grieved; he thought that Jesus doubted his love. He knew that his Lord had cause to distrust him, and with an aching heart he answered, 'Lord, Thou knowest all things; Thou knowest that I love Thee.' Again Jesus said to him, 'Feed My sheep.'

"Three times Peter had openly denied his Lord, and three times Jesus drew from him the assurance of his love and loyalty, pressing home that pointed question, like a barbed arrow to his wounded heart. Before the assembled disciples Jesus revealed the depth of Peter's repentance, and showed how thoroughly humbled was the once boasting disciple.

"Peter was naturally forward and impulsive, and Satan had taken advantage of these characteristics to overthrow him. Just before the fall of Peter, Jesus had said to him, 'Satan hath desired to have you, that he may sift you as wheat: but I have prayed for thee, that thy faith fail not: and when thou art converted, strengthen thy brethren.' Luke 22:31, 32. That time had now come, and the transformation in Peter was evident. The close, testing questions of the Lord had not called out one forward, self-sufficient reply; and because of his humiliation and repentance, Peter was better prepared than ever before to act as shepherd to the flock.

"The first work that Christ entrusted to Peter on restoring him to the ministry was to feed the lambs. This was a work in which Peter had little experience. It would require great care and tenderness, much patience and perseverance. It called him to minister to those who were young in the faith, to teach the ignorant, to open the Scriptures to them, and to educate them for usefulness in Christ's service. Heretofore Peter had not been fitted to do this, or even to understand its importance. But this was the work which Jesus now called upon him to do. For this work his own experience of suffering and repentance had prepared him.

"Before his fall, Peter was always speaking unadvisedly, from the impulse of the moment. He was always ready to correct others, and to express his mind, before he had a clear comprehension of himself or of what he had to say. But the converted Peter was very different. He retained his former fervor, but the grace of Christ regulated his zeal. He was no longer impetuous, self-confident, and self-exalted, but calm, self-possessed, and teachable. He could then feed the lambs as well as the sheep of Christ's flock.

"The Saviour's manner of dealing with Peter had a lesson for him and for his brethren. It taught them to meet the transgressor with patience, sympathy, and forgiving love. Although Peter had denied his Lord, the love which Jesus bore him never faltered. Just such love should the undershepherd feel for the sheep and lambs committed to his care. Remembering his own weakness and failure, Peter was to deal with his flock as tenderly as Christ had dealt with him.

"The question that Christ had put to Peter was significant. He mentioned only one condition of discipleship and service. 'Lovest thou Me?' He said. This is the essential qualification. Though Peter might possess every other, yet without the love of Christ he could not be a faithful shepherd over the Lord's flock. Knowledge, benevolence, eloquence, gratitude, and zeal are all aids in the good work; but without the love of Jesus in the heart, the work of the Christian minister is a failure" (*The Desire of Ages*, 811–815; see also *Messiah*, 433–435).

Questions to consider

1. How did Jesus show that Peter had truly repented of denying Him and had become humble? If you had seen Peter deny Jesus, would this have persuaded you that Peter had changed? Do you find it easy to forgive and start trusting others again?

2. How had Peter changed since His conversion? How did you change? What is the most dramatic conversion change you have witnessed?

_____

_____

3. What is the essential qualification for discipleship and service? Is that what we look for first in a minister or leader?

_____

_____

Reflect on the story

"Before Jesus' arrest, Peter had sworn to die for Him if necessary. But he failed even to stand up for Jesus. Someday he would have another opportunity to prove his love. To build his faith for that final test, Jesus talked to Peter about his future. After a life of working for his Savior, Peter would indeed have the chance to die for Him. Jesus told Peter, ' "When you are old, you will put out your hands and someone else will tie you and take you where you don't want to go" ' (John 21:18, NCV). Jesus saw that Peter's hands would be spread out on a cross. Once again, He told His disciple, 'Follow Me.'

"Peter wasn't discouraged to know this. He felt willing to suffer anything for his Lord. Before, Peter had loved Jesus as a man; now he loved Him as God. When he was led to a cross at the end of his life, Peter asked that he be crucified upside down. He thought it was too great an honor to die the same way his Master had.

"Always before, Peter had tried to plan God's work instead of waiting to follow God's plan. Jesus told him, 'Follow Me. Don't run ahead of Me. Let Me go ahead of you and you won't be defeated by the enemy.'

"As Peter walked beside Jesus along the shore, he glanced back to see John following them. Suddenly curious, he asked, 'Lord, what will happen to him?'

"Jesus shook His head and answered, 'If I want him to live until I come back, that isn't your concern. Just follow Me.' Jesus didn't say that John would live until the Second Coming. He said that even if that happened, it wouldn't affect Peter's work. Personal duty was what was required of each of them.

"Many people today are more interested in other people's business than their own. We should each be sure to look only at Jesus and follow Him. By watching Him, our lives will be changed.

"John lived to see Jerusalem destroyed and the temple demolished. To the end of his life, he followed Jesus faithfully.

"Peter was reinstated as an apostle, but Jesus did not give him any authority over the others. This was clear in His answer to Peter's question about John—'That isn't your concern. Just follow Me.' Peter was not placed in charge of the new church. He was a very influential leader, but the lesson Jesus taught him by the lake that day stayed with him the rest of his life.

"Later, in a letter to the churches, Peter reminded the leaders and elders that he had learned from Jesus how to care for His sheep. He said, 'Do not be like a ruler over people you are responsible for, but be good examples to them. Then when Christ, the Chief Shepherd, comes, you will get a glorious crown that will never lose its beauty' (1 Peter 5:3, 4, NCV)" (*Messiah,* 435, 436; see also *The Desire of Ages,* 815–817).

Questions to consider

1. Too often, Peter had tried to plan God's work instead of waiting to follow God's plan. How can we learn to wait for God's plans? How can we know when we are following God's plans?

2. What happened to Peter in the future? Did Jesus give Peter any authority over the other disciples or the church?

3. If we treated others the way Jesus treated Peter, how would our churches and homes be different?

"Meet Me in Galilee"   14

This study is based on Matthew 28:16–20 and
The Desire of Ages, chapter 86
—see also *Messiah,* chapter 86.

Jesus keeps His promise

The crowd scattered across the hillside in Galilee was larger than it seemed. Small groups buzzed as people excitedly discussed what had happened in Jerusalem since the crucifixion of Jesus. "I saw Him die with my own eyes! Can it be true that He is back?" "I heard that an angel told Peter that Jesus would meet Him here."

About five hundred believers had traveled to Galilee from all directions, traveling at night and by back roads to avoid being noticed by the Jewish leaders. As news of Jesus' resurrection spread to the believers who had gathered in Jerusalem for Passover, invitations to this gathering spread as well. Every person who believed in Jesus had done all they could to make it to the hillside.

"Thomas! Thomas! Is it really true? Have you seen Him?"

The disciples moved from group to group in the crowd, sharing their news and their experiences with the risen Savior. "I have seen Him—and touched Him just as I am touching you now," Thomas answered as he laid a hand on the questioner's arm. "He is just as He was before—only different."

Suddenly Jesus appeared in the middle of the crowd. The whispers hushed as every eye focused on Jesus. Many of the believers there had never before seen Jesus. But they had all heard the stories of His miracles, His teachings, and His death. When they saw the scars from the Crucifixion on His hands and feet, they accepted Him as the Savior and worshiped Him. But even there, some doubted that this was really Jesus.

"All power in heaven and earth has been given to Me," He said. These words, coming from the lips that they feared had been silenced forever, thrilled the believers with their authority. Many of them had seen Jesus heal the sick and drive out demons. He had quieted storms and walked on water. He had even raised the dead. But now, "all power" had been given to Him. Now they begin to see Him as He truly was—not a prophet or healer, but God in human form.

Jesus' words meant that His mission was complete. He had come to earth to live a perfect life in a sinful world. He had come to show the universe what His Father was really like. He had come to offer His life in payment for the sins of humans. Now His work was done.

But first, He gave His followers their mission: "Go and spread My message, and make new followers throughout the world. Baptize them, and teach them the things I taught you. And I will be with you until the world ends."

Jesus' first direction may have surprised them. "You must begin in Jerusalem." The headquarters of Jesus' enemies might be dangerous ground, but it was here that Jesus had offered His sacrifice. Here His teachings had been heard and repeated, touching many lives. Many people in Jerusalem secretly believed in Jesus, and many others had been misled by the priests and leaders.

The first ones to hear Jesus' offer of mercy and forgiveness would be the ones who murdered Him. But that would be only the beginning. From there the gospel would spread to the farthest reaches of the earth.

We may not have been there that day in Galilee, but we can still feel the power of Jesus' words and take our place in spreading His message.

Reflect on the story

"Through the gift of the Holy Spirit the disciples were to receive a marvelous power. Their testimony was to be confirmed by signs and wonders. Miracles would be wrought, not only by the apostles, but by those who received their message. Jesus said, 'In My name shall they cast out devils; they shall speak with new tongues; they shall take up serpents; and if they drink any deadly thing, it shall not hurt them; they shall lay hands on the sick, and they shall recover.' Mark 16:17, 18.

"At that time poisoning was often practiced. Unscrupulous men did not hesitate to remove by this means those who stood in the way of their ambition. Jesus knew that the life of His disciples would thus be imperiled. Many would think it doing God service to put His witnesses to death. He therefore promised them protection from this danger.

"The disciples were to have the same power which Jesus had to heal 'all manner of sickness and all manner of disease among the people.' By healing in His name the diseases of the body, they would testify to His power for the healing of the soul. Matthew 4:23; 9:6. And a new endowment was now promised. The disciples were to preach among other nations, and they would receive power to speak other tongues. The apostles and their associates were unlettered men, yet through the outpouring of the Spirit on the day of Pentecost, their speech, whether in their own or a foreign language, became pure, simple, and accurate, both in word and in accent.

"Thus Christ gave His disciples their commission. He made full provision for the prosecution of the work, and took upon Himself the responsibility for its success. So long as they obeyed His word, and worked in connection with Him, they could not fail. Go to all nations, He bade them. Go to the farthest part of the habitable globe, but know that My presence will be there. Labor in faith and confidence, for the time will never come when I will forsake you.

"The Saviour's commission to the disciples included all the believers. It includes all believers in Christ to the end of time. It is a fatal mistake to suppose that the work of saving souls depends alone on the ordained minister. All to whom the heavenly inspiration has come are put in trust with the gospel. All who receive the life of Christ are ordained to work for the salvation of their fellow men. For this work the church was established, and all who take upon themselves its sacred vows are thereby pledged to be co-workers with Christ.

" 'The Spirit and the bride say, Come. And let him that heareth say, Come.' Revelation 22:17. Everyone who hears is to repeat the invitation. Whatever one's calling in life, his first interest should be to win souls for Christ. He may not be able to speak to congregations, but he can work for individuals.

To them he can communicate the instruction received from his Lord. Ministry does not consist alone in preaching. Those minister who relieve the sick and suffering, helping the needy, speaking words of comfort to the desponding and those of little faith. Nigh and afar off are souls weighed down by a sense of guilt. It is not hardship, toil, or poverty that degrades humanity. It is guilt, wrongdoing. This brings unrest and dissatisfaction. Christ would have His servants minister to sin-sick souls.

"The disciples were to begin their work where they were. The hardest and most unpromising field was not to be passed by. So every one of Christ's workers is to begin where he is. In our own families may be souls hungry for sympathy, starving for the bread of life. There may be children to be trained for Christ. There are heathen at our very doors. Let us do faithfully the work that is nearest. Then let our efforts be extended as far as God's hand may lead the way. The work of many may appear to be restricted by circumstances; but, wherever it is, if performed with faith and diligence it will be felt to the uttermost parts of the earth. Christ's work when upon earth appeared to be confined to a narrow field, but multitudes from all lands heard His message. God often uses the simplest means to accomplish the greatest results. It is His plan that every part of His work shall depend on every other part, as a wheel within a wheel, all acting in harmony. The humblest worker, moved by the Holy Spirit, will touch invisible chords, whose vibrations will ring to the ends of the earth, and make melody through eternal ages.

"But the command, 'Go ye into all the world,' is not to be lost sight of. We are called upon to lift our eyes to the 'regions beyond.' Christ tears away the wall of partition, the dividing prejudice of nationality, and teaches a love for all the human family. He lifts men from the narrow circle which their selfishness prescribes; He abolishes all territorial lines and artificial distinctions of society. He makes no difference between neighbors and strangers, friends and enemies. He teaches us to look upon every needy soul as our brother, and the world as our field" (*The Desire of Ages,* 821–823; see also *Messiah,* 439–441).

Questions to consider

1. Jesus promised that the disciples would be able to perform miracles of healing and speak other languages. Does He promise the same today? Why do we not see more miraculous healings or speaking as part of evangelism?

2. Jesus "took responsibility" for the disciples' success in evangelism. Do we believe that He does the same today? What are we responsible for in evangelism?

3. Ministry is more than just preaching. In what ways have you been involved in ministry? In what ways would you like to be in the future?

4. Why is it often easier to do mission work somewhere away from our own homes or communities? What can we do to reach those closest to us?

Reflect on the story

"Jesus instructed His disciples to teach people to obey what He taught them. This includes what He taught through the prophets in the Old Testament. But it leaves no room for teaching traditions, human theories, or church laws. The Bible, the record of His own words and deeds, is the treasure we are to share with the world.

"The gospel should not be shared as a theory, but as a living force that changes lives. Jesus accepts even the most evil and hateful humans; then the gospel changes them. When they repent, He gives them His Holy Spirit and sends them back to their friends and acquaintances to show His life-changing love. Through His grace, humans can form a character like that of Jesus.

"Jesus' followers should present the story of His Gift—His love and sacrifice for us—in the most attractive way possible. The story of Jesus' wonderful love will melt hearts that will never respond to presentations of doctrine. Words alone cannot tell the story of that love—the storyteller's life must show it as well. Jesus is sitting for a portrait in every one of His followers. His love and His truth are being sketched onto each of our faces and hearts. In each of us, His patient love, His mercy, and His truth should shine out to the world.

"Those first disciples prepared themselves for their work. Before the Feast of Pentecost, they met together and settled all their arguments and worries. With single purpose and mind, they prayed in faith for those in the world around them. Then the Holy Spirit was given them without measure. As they preached with power, thousands were converted to Jesus in a single day.

"It can be the same way now. We should put away our disagreements and give ourselves to God's plan for saving those who are lost. We should ask with faith for the same blessing of the Holy Spirit, and it will come. The outpouring of the Holy Spirit on the apostles was called the 'early rain' and the results were amazing. But when the 'latter rain' falls in the last days, it will be even more glorious.

"Those who dedicate their body, soul, and mind to God will constantly receive new gifts of physical and mental power. By cooperating with Jesus, even weak humans will be allowed to do the works of God.

"The Savior longs to show His grace and stamp His character on the whole world. He wants to make humans free and pure and holy. Through His power, we will have victories over sin that will bring glory to God and to the Lamb. Jesus will see the results of His sacrifice and be satisfied" (*Messiah*, 441, 442; see also *The Desire of Ages*, 826–828).

Questions to consider

1. Have we learned the gospel as a theory, a set of teachings to research and agree to? How can it be a living force in our lives?

2. What will melt hearts and change lives like nothing else we can share? How can we share it with more than just words?

_____

_____

3. "Jesus is sitting for a portrait in every one of His followers." What does that mean to you?

_____

_____

Jesus Returns to Heaven 15

This study is based on Luke 24:50–53; Acts 1:9–12; and *The Desire of Ages,* chapter 87—see also *Messiah,* chapter 87.

"I will be with you always"

It was time. Jesus walked with His disciples toward the city gate, enjoying the bright sunshine. How people must have stared at the little group! Their religious leaders had just had that Man nailed to a cross! How many of those who stared had stood beneath the cross, jeering and shouting? How many had watched Him die? Their eyes followed Him out of the city, wondering with every step who He really was—and what would happen next.

Jesus had stayed on earth this long so that His disciples could get comfortable with Him in His glorified body. He could see that they no longer thought of His tomb every time they looked at Him. Now they saw Him as a King. Now they saw Him as God. So now it was time for Him to leave.

The disciples didn't know that these were their last moments with their Friend.

Jesus led them to a spot they had often visited together—the Mount of Olives. As they walked, Jesus repeated many of the things He had taught them. As they passed Gethsemane, He stopped and reminded them again: "I am the vine and you are the branches." He wanted them to remember how closely connected they would always be to Him and to His Father.

Jesus must have stopped to think about His life on earth. Born to poor parents, no aspect of His life had been easy. Even as a child, He was teased and criticized for being "too good." When His ministry began, people laughed at Him and insulted Him. They mocked Him, suggesting that He didn't even know who His father was. He was hated by many, rejected by most, and finally, crucified by those He had come to save.

Would He reject these thankless people, leaving them to suffer the fate they had chosen? Would He take back His loving concern, His offer to save them?

No. Instead, He promised, "I will be with you always."

Jesus led them to the area near Bethany, on the other side of the Mount of Olives. There He stopped and the eleven disciples gathered around Him as they had so many times before. In these last moments, Jesus didn't scold their lack of faith during His trials. He didn't remind them of their arrogance or how slow they had been to understand His plan. He spoke only encouraging words, words of love and assurance.

Then, in a familiar and reassuring way, He stretched out His arms to include them all in a blessing. As He assured them of His unending love, He slowly rose up from where He stood, drawn into the sky by a power stronger than gravity.

As Jesus rose higher, the disciples stared up after Him, standing on tiptoes and shielding their eyes for one last glimpse of their Friend. A glorious cloud seemed to move across the sky toward Him—soon they could see that it was a chariot of angels, come to greet their Lord. As they met Him, the disciples heard the joyful music of the angel choir as Jesus' last words floated down to their ears: "I will be with you always."

Reflect on the story

"While the disciples were still gazing upward, voices addressed them which sounded like richest music. They turned, and saw two angels in the form of men, who spoke to them, saying, 'Ye men of Galilee, why stand ye gazing up into heaven? this same Jesus, which is taken up from you into heaven, shall so come in like manner as ye have seen Him go into heaven.'

"These angels were of the company that had been waiting in a shining cloud to escort Jesus to His heavenly home. The most exalted of the angel throng, they were the two who had come to the tomb at Christ's resurrection, and they had been with Him throughout His life on earth. With eager desire all heaven had waited for the end of His tarrying in a world marred by the curse of sin. The time had now come for the heavenly universe to receive their King. Did not the two angels long to join the throng that welcomed Jesus? But in sympathy and love for those whom He had left, they waited to give them comfort. 'Are they not all ministering spirits, sent forth to minister for them who shall be heirs of salvation?' Hebrews 1:14.

"Christ had ascended to heaven in the form of humanity. The disciples had beheld the cloud receive Him. The same Jesus who had walked and talked and prayed with them; who had broken bread with them; who had been with them in their boats on the lake; and who had that very day toiled with them up the ascent of Olivet—the same Jesus had now gone to share His Father's throne. And the angels had assured them that the very One whom they had seen go up into heaven, would come again even as He had ascended. He will come 'with clouds; and every eye shall see Him.' 'The Lord Himself shall descend from heaven with a shout, with the voice of the Archangel, and with the trump of God: and the dead in Christ shall rise.' 'The Son of man shall come in His glory, and all the holy angels with Him, then shall He sit upon the throne of His glory.' Revelation 1:7; 1 Thessalonians 4:16; Matthew 25:31. Thus will be fulfilled the Lord's own promise to His disciples: 'If I go and prepare a place for you, I will come again, and receive you unto Myself; that where I am, there ye may be also.' John 14:3. Well might the disciples rejoice in the hope of their Lord's return.

"When the disciples went back to Jerusalem, the people looked upon them with amazement. After the trial and crucifixion of Christ, it had been thought that they would appear downcast and ashamed. Their enemies expected to see upon their faces an expression of sorrow and defeat. Instead of this there was only gladness and triumph. Their faces were aglow with a happiness not born of earth. They did not mourn over disappointed hopes, but were full of praise and thanksgiving to God. With rejoicing they told the wonderful story of Christ's resurrection and His ascension to heaven, and their testimony was received by many.

"The disciples no longer had any distrust of the future. They knew that Jesus was in heaven, and that His sympathies were with them still. They knew that they had a friend at the throne of God, and they were eager to present their requests to the Father in the name of Jesus. In solemn awe they bowed in prayer, repeating the assurance, 'Whatsoever ye shall ask the Father in My name, He will give it you. Hitherto have ye asked nothing in My name: ask, and ye shall receive, that your joy may be full.' John 16:23, 24. They extended the hand of faith higher and higher, with the mighty argument, 'It is Christ that died, yea rather, that is risen again, who is even at the right hand of God, who also maketh intercession for us.' Romans 8:34. And Pentecost brought them fullness of joy in the presence of the Comforter, even as Christ had promised" (*The Desire of Ages*, 831–833; see also *Messiah*, 444, 445).

Questions to consider

1. The two angels were the same ones who had been at Jesus' tomb, the same ones who had been with Him all His life on earth. Did Jesus have two guardian angels? What kindness did they show the disciples?

2. Jesus' promise to return was very real to the disciples who watched Him leave. How can it be real to us?

3. Why did the disciples no longer fear for the future? Can we also live with no fear of the future?

4. What made the disciples eager to present their requests to the Father? What can make us eager as well?

Reflect on the story

"All of heaven was waiting to welcome the Savior home. As He rose, He led the large group of prisoners set free from death and sin at His resurrection. When they came near the city of God, the angel escort called out a challenge:

Gates of heaven, open wide!
Open wide, ancient doors
So the glorious King can come in!

"With great joy the waiting angel guards responded: 'Who is this glorious King?' They knew who was coming—they just wanted to hear the answer of praise:

The Lord, strong and mighty,
The Lord, our Mighty Warrior!
Gates of heaven, open wide!

> Open wide, ancient doors
> So the glorious King can come home!

"Then the mighty gates of the city opened wide and the angel throng swept through with a burst of heavenly music. The commanders of the angel armies and the sons of God from other worlds had gathered to welcome home the Savior and to celebrate His victory.

"But Jesus waved them back. First He stepped up to His Father. He pointed to the healed wounds on His head, His side, and His feet. He lifted His hands, which still showed the marks of the nails. Then He presented the ones who had come to life with Him as representatives of the great numbers who will come from the grave at His second coming.

"Before the earth was created, Father and Son had joined hands in a solemn pledge that Jesus would become the Guarantor for the human race. When Jesus cried out from the cross, 'It is finished,' He was speaking to His Father. Their agreement had been carried out. Now He declared, 'Father, I have completed the work of redemption. I want the people that You gave Me to be with Me here.'

"The voice of God proclaimed that justice had been met, that Satan was defeated, that Jesus' struggling loved ones on earth were accepted. Then the Father threw His arms around His Son. The announcement was made, ' "Let all God's angels worship him" ' (Hebrews 1:6, NCV).

"With those words, heaven seemed to overflow with joy and praise. Love had conquered evil. Those who had been lost were now found. Heaven rang with choruses of voices proclaiming, ' "To the One who sits on the throne and to the Lamb be praise and honor and glory and power forever and ever" ' (Revelation 5:13, NCV).

"From that scene of joy in heaven, we hear the echo of Jesus' words, ' "I am going back to my Father and your Father, to my God and your God" ' (John 20:17, NCV). The family of heaven and the family of earth are now joined together forever. For us, Jesus—our Lord—our Messiah—rose, and for us He lives. 'So he is able always to save those who come to God through him because he always lives, asking God to help them' (Hebrews 7:25, NCV)" (*Messiah*, 445–447; see also *The Desire of Ages*, 833–835).

Questions to consider

1. The song welcoming Jesus home to heaven comes from Psalm 24:7–10. Read it in one or more versions of the Bible.

2. Name the groups who were there to greet the returning Jesus and celebrate His victory.

3. What did Jesus say to His Father? What did the voice of God proclaim as Jesus stood before Him?

4. What does it mean to you that Jesus is in heaven today, a human like you are?